AF600174

The Catholic University of America
Canon Law Studies
No. 205

THE MATRIMONIAL IMPEDIMENT OF NONAGE

AN HISTORICAL SYNOPSIS AND COMMENTARY

BY THE
Rev. John C. O'Dea, A.B., J.C.L.
PRIEST OF THE ARCHDIOCESE OF SAN FRANCISCO

A DISSERTATION

Submitted to the Faculty of the School of Canon Law of the Catholic University of America in Partial Fulfillment of the Requirements for the Degree of Doctor of Canon Law

THE CATHOLIC UNIVERSITY OF AMERICA PRESS
WASHINGTON, D. C.
1944

Nihil Obstat:

HIERONYMUS D. HANNAN, S.T.D., J.C.D.

Censor Deputatus

Washington D. C. die XII maii, 1944

Imprimatur:

✠ JOANNES J. MITTY, D.D.

Archiepiscopus Sancti Francisi

MURRAY & HEISTER—WASHINGTON, D. C.

PRINTED IN UNITED STATES

 9

MARIÆ
MATRI IMMACULATÆ

TABLE OF CONTENTS

FOREWORD

THIS work aims to be an analysis and treatment of the matrimonial impediment of nonage as it is established by the Church in her Code of Canon Law under canon 1067. The term, " impediment of nonage," is used in preference to the more commonly applied " impediment of age," as expressing more accurately and less ambiguously the true nature of the impediment.

While it is true that there are many moral, physiological and sociological implications in the question of the proper age for marriage, this phase of the problem will be treated only in so far as it has influenced the legislation of the Church, for the point of view and approach to the problem is directly canonical. Much that one must say in expounding the ecclesiastical impediment of nonage is bound to have but an academic value and interest, especially in this country where custom, educational standards, economic conditions, and indirectly civil legislation have affected a minimum age requisite for marriage higher than the diriment impediment instituted by the Church..

The ecclesiastical impediment is hardly a perplexing problem to the ordinary pastor in his care of souls, nor even to the diocesan tribunals in their phase of matrimonial problems. However, no marriage legislation of the Church can be considered unimportant. It is an age-old, reasoned and divinely guided wisdom and a deep concern for the well-being of her children, as individuals and as members of society, that has prompted every item of her marriage law. No one canon stands alone. It has a relationship to many other laws. To see the relationship leads to a better understanding of the law, which is the purpose of this canonical study.

The writer wishes to take this occasion to express his sincere gratitude to the Most Reverend John J. Mitty, D.D., Archbishop of San Francisco, for the opportunity to pursue graduate study in Canon Law; to the faculty of the School of Canon Law of the Catholic University of America for their aid and encouragement; and to all others who contributed to the completion of this work.

CHAPTER I

Historical Summary

To trace back and search out the source and origin of any law of the Church is not merely a matter of historical interest, but of practical canonical import as well; for to understand completely, to interpret properly and to appreciate fully the meaning of present-day legislation its relation to the past must be considered.[1] With this in mind much of the history of the Church's law on the age required for marriage and the corresponding impediment of nonage will be integrated with the canonical treatment of the current law. But it does seem advisable by way of introduction to trace back in outline the origin of the impediment. The approach is that of a review, beginning with the law as it was immediately preceding the enactment of the new Code, working back through the Council of Trent, the Decretal Collections, and Gratian to Roman Law.

Article 1: *Impediment of Nonage Previous to the Code*

The essential note of the impediment of nonage prior to the new law of the Code was an identification of the age required for marriage with the age of puberty and the impeding from marriage of those who had not attained to that state of physical and moral development. But the attainment of puberty was based not on the physiological fact verified in each individual case, but rather on a presumption of law which considered that a boy had attained the age of puberty when he completed his fourteenth year, and the girl upon the completion of her twelfth year.[2]

---

[1] Cf. canon 6.

[2] Feije, *De Impedimentis et Dispensationibus Matrimonialibus* (3. ed., Lovanii, 1885), n. 551; Wernz, *Ius Decretalium* (6 vols., Romae et Prati, 1898–1905), Vol. IV, *Ius Matrimoniale Ecclesiae Catholicae* (1904), n. 309 (hereafter cited as *Ius Matrimoniale*); Gasparri, *Tractatus Canonicus de Matrimonio* (3. ed., 2 vols., Parisiis, 1904), I, n. 545 (hereafter cited as *De Matrimonio*).

But the impediment of nonage was not absolute, since it was based on a *praesumptio iuris tantum.*[3] If it could be satisfactorily proved that actual puberty, that is, the *potentia generandi* and the *debita mentis discretio,* was actually attained by the boy before the completion of his fourteenth year, or by the girl before the completion of her twelfth year, then the presumption yielded to the fact and the party could enter upon a valid marriage. It was the attainment of puberty and the precocious physical and moral maturity before the legally presumed age of puberty that fulfilled the condition of *malitia supplet aetatem.*[4]

By the strict rigor of the law, when this condition was fulfilled a person could marry. Such a marriage was then valid and could never be proved null on the grounds of lack of age.[5] However, for licitness that was not enough. It was necessary that the ordinary of the place or the Holy See pass judgment on the fulfillment of the conditions, verify the facts and give permission for the marriage to take place, if the legal age had not been completed, but actually puberty had been attained.[6]

This then was the law on the impediment of nonage prior to the change made by the new Code. In virtue of canon 10 which rules that laws do not have a retroactive effect,[7] and especially in view of the response from the Commission on the Interpretation

[3] Sanchez, *Disputationum de Sancto Matrimonii Sacramento Tomi Tres* (Antverpiae, 1626), lib. VII, disp. 104, n. 4 (hereafter cited as *De Matrimonio*). Hostiensis, *In Quinque Libros Decretalium Commentaria* (5 vols. in 3, Venetiis, 1581), lib. IV, tit. II, c. 3, s.v. *ostendit* (hereafter cited as Commentaria).

[4] Fagnanus, *Commentaria super Quinque Libros Decretalium* (5 vols. in 3, Venetiis, 1661), lib. IV, tit. II, n. 3 (hereafter cited as *Commentaria*).

[5] De Justis, *De Dispensationibus Matrimonialibus* (Lucae, 1726), lib. III, cap. VIII, n. 56.

[6] Benedictus XIV, litt. ap. "*Magnae Nobis,*" 29 iun. 1748—*Codicis Iuris Canonici Fontes cura Emi Petri Card. Gasparri Editi* (9 vols., Romae: Typis Polyglottis Vaticanis, 1923–1939, Vols. VII–IX *ed. cura et studio Emi. Iustiniani Card. Serédi*), n. 387 (hereafter cited as *Fontes*); *Collectanea S. Congregationis de Propaganda Fide* (2 vols., Romae: Typographia Polyglotta S. C. de Prop. Fide, 1907), n. 364 (hereafter cited as *Collectanea S. C. P. F.*).

[7] Canon 10.—Leges respiciunt futura, non praeterita, nisi nominatim in eis de praeteritis caveatur.

of the Code that the Code has no retroactive force even as regards impediments to marriage, and that marriages are to be governed by the law as it existed when they were contracted,[8] it must be this law that is applied in judging any marriage involving the impediment of nonage that took place prior to May 19, 1918.

In tracing back the origin and source of this law, it is of interest to note the statement of the impediment as found in the Austrian Instruction drawn up by Cardinal Rauscher (1797–1875), Archbishop of Vienna (1853–1875). However, this Instruction is not cited as a source of law, but rather as an officially sanctioned repetition of existing law for the Archdiocese of Vienna.[9] It was not universally applicable, but it deserves mentioning in so far as it was recommended for use in the United States by the Fathers of the III Plenary Council of Baltimore (1884).[10]

The Instruction lists the impediment under title of *Impubertas,* indicating the fact that boys who have not completed their fourteenth year, and girls their twelfth year, are considered by laws as incapable of marriage, but if it ever happens—the words carry the implication of a strong doubt—that they have the physical and moral aptitude for marriage before those ages, they still cannot marry without first obtaining a declaratory sentence to that effect from the bishop of the diocese or from the Holy See itself.[11]

---

[8] Pont. Cod. Com., 3 iun. 1918, IV, 6—*Acta Apostolicae Sedis, Commentarium Officiale* (Romae: 1909–), X (1918), 346 (hereafter cited as *AAS*); Bouscaren, *The Canon Law Digest* (2 vols., Milwaukee: The Bruce Publishing Co., Vol. I, 1934; Vol. II, 1943) I, 496.

[9] Cf. Wanenmacher, *Canonical Evidence in Marriage Cases,* The Catholic University of America Canon Law Studies, n. 9 (Philadelphia: Dolphin Press, 1935), p. xiv.

[10] *Acta et Decreta Concilii Plenarii Baltimorensis Tertii,* A.D.M.D.CCC-LXXXIV (Baltimore, 1886), n. 304: "Utiliter etiam poterit Instructio pro judiciis ecclesiasticis Imperii Austriaci in causis matrimonialibus, a. 1855 a gravibus theologicis et canonistis Romanis, licet solo privato suo judicio, commendata."

[11] Impedimenta Dirimentia, No. 17—"Impubertas: Quum pueri, qui decimum quartum, et puellae, quae duodecimum aetatis nondum absolverint, de regula neque physice ad matrimonium apti, neque ii sint, qui matrimonii contrahendi vim, prout decet, intelligant, de jure ad matrimonium inhabiles censentur.

Since, however, it is the origin and source of the Church's law on the impediment of nonage, and not the details of the law itself, which will be dealt with in the subsequent chapters, the commentary of the classical canonists and the various responses from the Holy See can be passed over at this point in order that the action of the Fathers of the Council of Trent (1545–1563) on the impediment of nonage may be considered.

ARTICLE 2: *The Council of Trent and the Age of Marriage*

At the twenty-fourth session of the Council of Trent, which treated the question of marriage, the consideration of the age at which persons could enter marriage was introduced. There was an attempt made to alter the existing law in regard to defect of age and to make necessary the presence of parental consent. In the decree first submitted to the assembled members of the Council on July 20, 1563, it was proposed to declare invalid the marriage contracted by a boy under 18 or by a girl under 16 unless he or she had parental consent.[12]

While it is true that the proposed decree dealt with the question of parental consent as well as that of the age of the parties themselves, yet the various voices and votes that approved or challenged this proposed decree touched on the subject of age. Some of those present at the Council favored still a more advanced age before sons or daughters could by their own free choice enter valid marriage. Thus the Cardinal Charles De Guise of Lorraine

---

Quodsi autem umquam eveniret, ut hac aetate minores et physica et morali ad matrimonium aptitudine pollerent, nihilominus, nisi desuper ab episcopo dioecesano vel ab ipsa Apostolica Sede sententiam declaratoriam obtinuerint, matrimonio jungi non possent."—*Acta et Decreta Sacrorum Conciliorum Recentiorum, Collectio Lacensis* (7 vols., Friburgi Brisgoviae: Herder and Co., 1870–1890), V, 1287 (hereafter cited as *Coll. Lac.*); *Analecta Iuris Pontificii* (Romae, 1855–1868, Parisiis, 1869–1891), II (1857), col. 2516.

[12] Decretum de clandestinis matrimoniis (propositum examinandi): ". . . insuper eadem sacrosancta synodus ea quoque matrimonia quae filii familiae ante decimum octavum, filiae vero ante decimum sextum suae aetatis annum completum, sine parentum consensu de cetero contraxerint, praesenti decreto irritat et annullat. . . ."—*Concilii Tridentini Diariorum, Actorum, Epistolarum Tractatuum Nova Collectio* (ed. Societas Görresiana, 13 vols., Friburgi Brisgoviae: B. Herder, 1901–1938), IX, 639.

(1524–1574), France, advocated that the age for women should be advanced to twenty years, and that of men to twenty-five.[13] The bishop of Cordia, Spain, Didacus de Almansa, expressed the opinion that the age for marriage should be twenty for women and twenty-two for men.[14] But the majority of those voting at the Council did not favor the decree as it was proposed, nor did they deem it advisable or reasonable to change the existing law on the age of marriage, or to make parental consent necessary. The Bishop of Ypres, Belgium, Martin Balduini, in his vote remarked that the part of the proposed decree regarding age did not meet with his approval, since it was against the counsel of the Apostle who said: " He who cannot practice self-control, let him marry." [15] The Bishop of Palermo, Joannes Bervaldus, gave as his reason for opposing any change that forbidding marriage until a more advanced age would be an occasion for fornication.[16] The Archbishop of Rossano, Paulus Verallus, in Italy, likewise thought that a change in the law would not be in keeping with the apostolic doctrine.[17]

The final outcome, then, at the Council of Trent in relation to the minimum age at which marriage could be contracted and the correlative impediment of nonage was negative. The Decree *Tametsi* and the canons of the twenty-fourth session on the reformation of marriage, as they were formally adopted and

[13] D. Card. Lotharingus: ". . . Deinde circa aetatem matrimonii contrahendi deberet reduci aetas mulierum ad vigesimum annum, virorum autem ad vigesimum quintum annum."—*op. cit.*, IX, 643.

[14] Episcopus Cauriensis: ". . . aetas sit vigesimum et vigesimum duos."—*op. cit.*, IX, 659.

[15] Episcopus Hyprensis: ". . . quoad aetatem, non placet, quia est contra consilium apostoli qui ait: 'Quin non potest continere, nubat,' videlicet in quacumque aetate et etiam invito patre. Neque etiam adversandum naturali libertati."—*op. cit.*, IX, 669.

[16] Episcopus Panormitanus: ". . . quod aetatem servetur jus commune ne demus causam fornicationum . . . Non est igitur arctanda aetas."—*op. cit.*, p. 664.

[17] Archiepiscopus Rossanensis: ". . . Divina et apostolica doctrina dicit: Si non potes caste vivere, nube. Doctrina nostra dicat; Si non potes caste vivere, non nubas, nisi parentes consentiant . . . Matrimonium datum est ad remedium concupiscentiae, si remedium coarctamus, morbum vero coarctare non possumus."—*op. cit.*, IX, 694.

approved, were silent on the question of age. But the Council did anathematize those who contended that parental consent was necessary for the valid or licit marriage of sons or daughters.[18]

ARTICLE 3: *The Age of Marriage as Found in the "Corpus Iuris Canonici"*

Since the Council of Trent did not change the law either on the age required for marriage or regarding the impediment of nonage, it was the former legislation, that is, the law of the *Corpus Iuris Canonici* that still retained its binding force. It is especially in the Decretal Collection (1234) of Pope Gregory IX (1227–1241) that the salient points of the law on the age of marriage can be traced. In this authentic collection, the second title of the fourth book, *De desponsatione impuberum,* contains much that is relevant.

In the second chapter of that title a decree of Pope St. Nicholas I (858–867) is given in which he strictly forbade marriage when one or both of the parties had not arrived at the age determined by the laws and the canons, except for a most serious reason such as the promotion of peace.[19] Worthy of special note in this chapter of the Decretals is the reference to another system of law (Roman law) and the fact that the strict prohibition, the impediment to marriage below the prescribed age, can yield when a sufficiently grave reason of a public nature arises.

Following this, the Decretals give an excerpt from the *Etymologiae* of St. Isidore (Ca. 560–636), in which puberty as a condition for marriage is defined and explained. It is stated that some estimate puberty from the number of years attained, and

---

[18] *Op. cit.,* IX, 968; Conc. Trident., sess. XXIV, *de ref. matrim.,* c. 1.

[19] C. 2, X, *de desponsatione impuberum,* IV, 2 (Nicolaus Papa), "Ubi non est consensus: (et infra) huius ergo decreti auctoritate districtius inhibemus, ne aliqui, quorum uterque vel alter ad aetatem legibus vel canonibus determinatam non perverit coniungantur, nisi forte aliqua urgentissima necessitate interveniente, utpote pro bono pacis, talis coniunctio toleretur."—*Corpus Iuris Canonici* (ed. Lipiensis 2. post curas Aemili Ludovici Richeteri instruxit Aemilius Friedberg, 2 vols., Lipsiae; Tauchnitz, 1879–1881; ed. anastatice repetita, 2 vols., Lipsiae, 1928); cf. *Compilatio* I, c. 4, *h. t.,* IV, 2—*Quinque Compilationes Antiquae* (Friedberg's ed., Lipsiae, 1882).

consider one as *pubes* when he has completed his fourteenth year, even though actual puberty is attained later, but that in reality puberty can be certainly ascertained from the bodily appearances and by the actual presence of the powers of generation.[20]

But it is especially in the Decretal law that the conditional nature of the impediment of nonage can be traced. There are responses from Pope Alexander III (1159–1181) to that effect. In giving the solution to a case submitted by the Bishop of Norwich, this pope made it clear that the age of marriage was not absolute, and that marriage contracted by a party who was below the legal age was not automatically null. Valid consent could be given in spite of the lack of years. The specific case was this: a certain girl already married sought permission to marry another, claiming that she did not give proper consent in the first marriage, since she was below the marriageable age at that time. But the pope pointed out that such permission for a new marriage was not to be given her, and that she was not to be separated from her husband. The circumstances that determined the decision were that the parents of the girl previous to her marriage had deceitfully asserted that she was of legal age; the husband had made a sworn statement to the effect that he had had carnal relations with her, and moreover she was proximate to the age of marriage, that is, in her eleventh year or about twelve at the time of the marriage.[21] In view of this papal response the capability of performing the marriage act and one's proximity to the legal age of marriage were considered sufficient to make up for the lack of age.

---

[20] C. 3, X, *de desponsatione impuberum,* IV, 2 (*Isidorii Etymologiae,* XI, 2; cf. *Compilatio* I, c. 7, *h. t.,* IV, 2): "Puberes a pube sunt vocati, id est a pudentia corporis nuncupati; quia haec loca prima lanuginem ducunt. Quidam tamen ex annis pubertatem aestimant, id est, eum esse puberem, qui XIV. annos implevit quamvis tardissime pubescat. Certum autem est, eum puberem esse, qui ex habitu corporis pubertatem ostendit, et generare iam potest. Et puerperae sunt, quae in annis puerilibus pariunt."

[21] C. 6, X, *de desponsatione impuberum,* IV, 2; cf. *Compilatio* I, c. 8, *h. t.,* IV, 2; Jaffé, *Regesta Romanorum Pontificum ab condita Ecclesia ad annum post Christum natum* MCMCVIII (2. ed. correctam et auctam auspiciis Guilielmi Wattenbach curaverunt S. Loewenfeld, F. Kaltenbrunner, P. Ewald, 2 vols. in 1, Lipsiae, 1885–1888), n. 14032 (hereafter cited as Jaffé).

To the Bishop of Bath in England, Pope Alexander III issued a similar decree emphasizing the fact that the "*carnalis commixtio*" can make an indissoluble marriage of an agreement that existed merely as *sponsalia de futuro,* even though the parties were not of marriageable age. The carnal relations between the parties seemed to indicate sufficient maturity and made up for the defect of years.[22]

The Archbishop of Genoa sought a papal decision on a case involving a couple who had married while they were still below the legal age, and who later sought a divorce alleging as their grounds the lack of age and the presence of parental force. Pope Alexander III responded that they were not to be separated on the first grounds if they were so near the legal age that they were capable of the *copula carnalis* and if at the same time it appeared that they had consented, since in that case "*malitia supplevisse aetatem videatur.*" But on the grounds of forced consent the question of age was not to be considered, for such force could nullify a marriage at any age, unless consent was given after the force was discontinued.[23] It is this decretal which appears to reflect the origin, in application to the age of marriage, of the principle: "*nisi malitia supplet aetatem.*"

However, a decretal from Pope Urban III (1185–1187) declared that merely an attempted consummation of a marriage contracted before the party had completed the necessary legal age for marriage was not enough to make it a valid marriage, if one of the parties was physically unable to consummate it. A boy not yet twelve years old had married. While both parties confessed that an attempt was made at consummation, yet the woman claimed that her virginity was not deflowered. When he was seventeen the boy refused to accept the woman. Upon proof that after the age of fourteen, the determined marriageable age, he did not give consent, both parties were declared free to contract

---

[22] C. 8, X, *de desponsatione impuberum,* IV, 2; cf. *Compilatio* I, c. 10, *h. t.,* IV, 2; Jaffé, n. 13765.

[23] C. 9, X, *de desponsatione impuberum,* IV, 2; cf. *Compilatio* I, c. 12, *h.t.,* IV, 2; Jaffé, n. 13969.

another marriage.[24] Defect of age and of physical capacity for marriage had a definite invalidating effect.

From a decretal of Pope Innocent III (1198–1216), it was clear that even though a boy and girl had expressed mutual consent *per verba de praesenti,* yet if either party was below the marriageable age and *prudentia* did not supply for age, then the contract was not that of marriage but only an engagement (*sponsalia*).[25] This same point was again stressed by Pope Boniface VIII (1294–1303) in his decretal collection. If one or both of the parties to a marriage were below the age of puberty, and not near that age, and in them *prudentia* did not supply for the defect of age, even though they expressed consent "*de praesenti*" and intended to contract marriage, they nevertheless contracted only *sponsalia de futuro.* The mere passing of time and their arrival at the age of puberty did not make the contract to be that of marriage, unless "*copula carnalis*" or some other equally indicative factor indicated that their intention remained unaltered.[26]

Previous to the Decretal, the Decree of Gratian (1140) did not give any special treatment to the subject of the age of marriage. In that section in which marriage is considered it is mentioned that *sponsalia* cannot be contracted before the age of seven.[27] While Gratian did not make any clear-cut distinction between *sponsalia de futuro* and *sponsalia de presenti,*[28] it seems obvious that the age here referred to was not for marriage itself, but rather for a promise of a future marriage.

---

[24] C. 10, X, *de desponsatione impuberum,* IV, 2; cf. *Compilatio* I, c. 13, *h.t.,* IV, 2; Jaffé, n. 15730.

[25] C. 14, X, *de desponsatione impuberum,* IV, 2; cf. *Compilatio* III, c. 2, *h.t.,* IV, 2; Potthast, *Regesta Pontificum Romanorum inde ab anno post Christum natum MCXCVIII ad annum MCCCIV* (2 vols. in 1, Berolini, 1874–1875), n. 2775 (hereafter cited as Potthast).

[26] C. 1, *de sponsalibus et matrimoniis,* IV, 1, in VI°.

[27] C. un., C.XXX, q. 2. "Sponsalia ante septennium contrahi non possunt. Solo enim consensu contrahuntur, qui intervenire non potest, nisi ab alterutra parte id intelligatur, quod inter eas agitur. Probantur ergo sponsalia non posse contrahi inter pueros, quorum aetatis infirmitas consensum non admittit."

[28] Cf. Wernz, *Ius Matrimoniale,* n. 460.

Gratian, however, did touch upon the subject of the age of marriage when he dealt with religious profession. The practice of children entering a monastery or convent at an early age, as well as being placed there by their parents, gave rise to the serious problem of the individual's freedom in the serious step of vowing virginity. It was determined that if a child had voluntarily entered a monastery, without a confirmation of that choice through parental consent, the profession of virginity did not bind until the child had reached adult age, at which time he or she was free to remain or to depart in dependence of his or her own choice in the matter.[29] This age was considered as present when one had arrived in his adult years, that is, when one had reached the age regarded as perfectly fitted for the purpose of marriage.[30] It may be gathered from a letter of Pope St. Gregory I (590-604) which Gratian quoted that the adult age in question was that of puberty.[31] Such is the argument which Bernard of Pavia († 1216) employed in deducing the age of marriage from Gratian.[32]

Moreover, the fact that Gratian insisted that consummation was of necessity required for a perfect marriage [33] made it likewise necessary for him to maintain that the actual attainment of puberty was required for a perfect marriage.

---

[29] C. 1, C. XX, q. 1. "Quod intra annos pueritiae traditi, cum adulti fuerint, liberum habeant manendi vel discedendi, probatur auctoritate nonae Sinodi . . ."

[30] *Loc. cit.:* "Firma autem tunc erit professio virginitatis, ex quo adulta iam aetas esse ceperit, et quae solet apta nuptiis deputari et perfecta."

[31] C. 2, C. XX, q. 1 (*Greg. I ad Augustinum Anglorum Episcoporum*—Jaffé, n. 1988) "Addidisti adhuc, quod si pater vel mater filium filiave intra septa monasterii in infantiae annis sub regulari tradiderunt disciplina, utrum liceat eis postquam ad pubertatis inoleverunt annos, egredi et matrimonio copulari. Hoc omnino devitamus, quia nefas est, ut oblatis a parentibus Deo filiis voluptatis frena relaxentur."

[32] Bernardus Papiensis, Summa Decretalium (ed. E.A.T. Laspeyres, Ratisbonae, 1861), lib. IV, tit. I: "Aetas apta nuptiis est in puella XII, in puero XIV annorum, quod colligitur ex C.XX, q. 1 et 2."

[33] C. 34, C.XXVII, q. 2. ". . . Sed sciendum est, quod coniugium desponsatione initiatur, commixtione perficitur. Unde inter sponsum et sponsam coniugium est, sed initiatum; inter copulatos est coniugium ratum."

ARTICLE 4: *Roman Law Source of the Law on the Age of Marriage*

But the Decretals themselves,[34] and especially the "*glossae*" to Gratian and the Decretals clearly indicate that the main stream of influence on the Church's law in regard to the age of marriage was the Roman Law. In this particular instance the Church adopted and canonized the prescriptions of the civil law that were in effect at the time of her institution and early development. Because these concepts were reasonable and not opposed to her divinely revealed fundamental principles regarding marriage, they could be readily accepted.

In Roman Law it was specifically determined that puberty was the minimum age at which a legitimate marriage (*iustae nuptiae*) could take place.[35] If marriage was attempted before that age the parties were not legitimately married until they later attained the necessary age.[36]

In the matter of determining when puberty was reached there existed two schools of legal thought among the early Romanists. Longinus Vassius (c. 3–75) and his followers maintained that the age of puberty depended completely on the physical development, that is, on whether the person was capable of generation. Hence physical inspection was necessary to determine the fact of puberty. But Sempronius Proculus, who flourished in the time of the Emperor Nero, and his followers maintained that when the boy had completed his fourteenth year that fact gave rise to a presumption which afforded sufficient certainty and that physical inspection was therefore not necessary.[37]

This controversy was settled by the Emperor Justinian (527–565), who legislated that physical inspection was unbecoming, and that puberty was always to be presumed when the boy had

---

[34] C. 2, X, *de desponsatione impuberum,* IV, 2.

[35] Inst. (1. 10).

[36] D. (23. 2) 4.

[37] Ulpianus XI, 29: "Liberantur tutela masculi quidem pubertate. Puberem autem Cassini quidem eum esse dicunt qui habitu corporis pubes apparet, i.e., qui generare possit. Proculeiani autem eum qui quattuor decem annos explevit."—*The Institutes of Gaius and the Rules of Ulpian* (ed. James Muirhead, Edinburg, 1904), p. 387.

completed his fourteenth year and the girl her twelfth year.[38] It was this presumption that appears to be the basis for the ecclesiastical law on the age of marriage and regarding the impediment of nonage. From Roman Law it was adopted and canonized, remaining in effect up until the Code introduced the new law.

The expression of the condition in the pre-Code impediment of nonage: "*nisi malitia supplet aetatem,*" can likewise be traced to Roman Law. However, it did not have application to marriage, but in its original context it denied the favor of law to those youths who, with the intent of deceiving, alleged that they were no longer bound by *tutela,* hence were free to make a contract, and then later claimed the fact that they were still *impuberes* to demand restitution.[39]

---

[38] D. (26,1); C. (5, 60).

[39] C. (2,42) 3.

CHAPTER II

The Nature of the Impediment of Nonage

Article 1: *Requisite Mental Capacity*

By the power that is hers by divine constitution, it lies within the competence of the supreme authority of the Church to regulate the contracting of marriage for her subjects. This is not only a point of law,[1] but also a dogma of faith.[2] The Church may do this, not by touching the nature of marriage, as a contract or as a sacrament, since these are of divine law, natural and positive, but rather by establishing impediments, that is, by determining external circumstances which make the person juridically incapable of marriage, or which gravely forbid one from licitly contracting marriage. It is this that the Church has done in regard to the age at which her subjects are capable of entering a valid marriage. Thus canon 1067:

1. Vir ante decimum sextum aetatis annum completum, mulier ante decimum quartum item completum, matrimonium validum inire non possunt.
2. Licet matrimonium post praedictum aetatem contractum validum sit, curent tamen animarum pastores ab eo avertere iuvenes ante aetatem, qua secundum regionis receptos mores, matrimonium inire solet.

1. " A male before the completion of the sixteenth year and a female before the completion of the fourteenth year cannot marry validly."

[1] Canon 1016.—Baptizatorum matrimonium regitur iure non solum divino, sed etiam canonico, salva competentia civilis potestatis circa mere civiles eiusdem matrimonii effectus.

Canon 1038. §1. Supremae tantum auctoritatis ecclesiasticae est authentice declarare quandonam ius divinum matrimonium impediat vel dirimat. §2. Eidem supremae auctoritati privative ius est alia impedimenta matrimonium impedientia vel dirimentia pro baptizatis constituendi per modum legis sive universalis sive particularis.

[2] Conc. Trident., sess. XXIV, *de matrimonio,* can. 3, 4, 9.

2. "Although marriage is valid after the completion of the above mentioned age, nevertheless pastors of souls should take care to deter from it young people who have not reached the age at which, according to the customs of the country, marriage is usually contracted." [3]

It must be noted from the outset that the present legislation of the Church on the age of marriage and the impediment of nonage as expressed in the canon has a twofold aspect. It sets up a minimum below which no subject of the Church may enter a valid marriage. This the Church has done by instituting a diriment impediment which directly affects the person so as to make him or her incapable of contracting marriage validly. But the second part of the law, and equally a part of it, is a strong directive norm for the pastors of souls. While emphasizing by repetition that the minimum age is sufficient for a valid marriage, nevertheless there is imposed an obligation on the pastors to dissuade from entering marriage those who have not attained the customary age of the particular locality. The Church is not canonizing local custom or civil law to the same extent as it does in the case of legal adoption [4] by making it an impediment, but it does wish to prevent its subject from marrying below an age which the reasonable custom, which reflects practice of a particular location in view of the social, moral, climatic conditions, dictates. While the emphasis throughout this work will be on nonage as a diriment impediment, that is, the minimum age at which marriage can validly be contracted, it must be borne in mind that the impediment is establishing a minimum age and in no wise is recommending this age as a desideratum. This point will receive fuller consideration later in this chapter.[5]

By Canon 1067 the Church has constituted the lack of the specifically determined age of sixteen years for men and fourteen years for women as a circumstance which impedes her subjects

[3] Translation from Ayrinac-Lydon, *Marriage Legislation in the New Code of Canon Law* (new, revised edition, New York: Benziger Brothers, 1938), p. 124.

[4] Canons 1059; 1080.

[5] Cf. *infra*, p. 25.

from marriage and makes them juridically incapable of expressing a valid matrimonial consent. Primarily, then, the impediment of nonage is one of ecclesiastical law. This is a cardinal point on which will hinge many conclusions. Its demonstration will serve the added purpose of showing the true nature of the impediment. By examining the constitutive and essential elements of marriage, and the minimum requirements under the natural law independent of any specification by competent authority for entering it, the point in question becomes clear.

That marriage is a contract [6] made by the consent of a man and a woman, and that consent consists in the act of the will of these parties in handing over and accepting mutually the right over the bodies of each other for the performance of the acts which are of themselves indicated and suited by nature for the generation of children, form the constitutive element of marriage is recognized not only in the canonical concept [7] but also in the natural law concept as well. Thus Cronin [8] defines marriage as " a stable union of persons of the opposite sexes, made under contract, with a view principally to the birth and rearing of children." He continues: " In this definition are contained the bare essentials of marriage, i.e. the elements that are required not for marriage at its best, but for marriage simply. It represents the least number of conditions required both in regard to the union itself and the purpose to which the union is directed." [9] In a similar manner Joyce [10] describes the natural law concept of marriage: ". . . by a law of nature so evident that only the deepest degradation can render men blind to it, marriage is a

---

[6] Marriage is here considered *in fieri,* that is, actively or causally as the contract which initiates and constitutes the conjugal society, as distinct from marriage *in facto esse,* the conjugal union itself, the state or bond of marriage, effected by the conjugal contract. Cappello, *Tractus Canonico-Moralis De Sacramentis,* 3 vols. in 6, Vol. III, *De Matrimonio* (ed. quarta emendata et aucta, Romae: Officina Libraria Marietti, 1939), n. 2 (hereafter cited as *De Sacramentis*).

[7] Cf. canons 1012; 1081.

[8] *The Science of Ethics* (2 vols., Dublin: H. M. Gill, 1922), II, 389.

[9] *Loc. cit.*

[10] *Christian Marriage,* Heythrop Series: I (London and New York: Sheed and Ward, 1933), p. 1.

stable contractual union freely embraced by man and woman having in view primarily the birth and rearing of children, and secondarily the reciprocal services of domestic life."

The notion, then, of marriage as a contract made by the consent of the parties brings with it some minimum demands as to when it can be contracted; for by natural law no contract of any kind can be made except by those who have a sufficient use of reason to understand the obligations which they assume. There must be free consent by which a right is transferred and an obligation undertaken.[11] Except with proper consent, human rights are not transferred by human beings who live under the law of reason. Since marriage implies the transfer of important rights and the assuming of serious obligations, the consent of both parties is necessary.[12]

But before consent can be given, at least some knowledge of the essential features of marriage and of the marriage contract in the contracting parties is required by the natural law. Psychologically consent without knowledge is impossible according to the accepted principle, *nil volitum, nisi praecognitum.*[13] To require, as the Church does,[14] that in order to give proper consent those who contract marriage be not ignorant that marriage is a permanent society between a man and a woman for the procreation of children does not seem to be overstepping the bounds of natural law, nor exceeding its essential and minimum requirements. As

---

[11] Tanquerey, *Synopsis Theologicae Moralis et Pastoralis* (3 vols., Vol. I, ed. duodecima, 1936; Vol. II, ed. nona, 1931; Vol. III, ed. decima, 1937, Parisiis: Decsclée et Socii.), III, n. 631; Gasparri, *Tractus Canonicus de Matrimonio* (ed. nova ad mentem Codicis I. C., 2 vols., Romae; Typis Polyglottis Vaticanis, 1932), II, n. 783 (hereafter this edition will be cited unless otherwise noted).

[12] Cf. canon 1081, § 1; Gasparri, *op. cit.* II, n. 775; Doheny, *Canonical Procedure in Matrimonial Cases* (Milwaukee: The Bruce Publishing Co., 1938), p. 498.

[13] Tanquerey, *op. cit.* II, n. 124; Chelodi, *Ius Matrimoniale iuxta Codicem Iuris Canonici* (3. ed., Trento: Libreria Moderna Editrice A. Ardesi et C., 1921), n. 108 (hereafter cited as *De Matrimonio*).

[14] C. 1082, § 1. Ut matrimonialis consensus haberi possit, necesse est ut contrahentes saltem non ignorent matrimonium esse societatem permanentem inter virum et mulierem ad filios procreandos.

Gasparri remarks: " [for matrimonial consent] the mere use of reason is not sufficient, but a discretion and maturity of judgment proportional to the contract is required so that the one contracting can understand the nature and force of the contract, otherwise he cannot consent to it . . . Hence that marriage be valid by the very law of nature, each party must so enjoy the use of reason so that he can sufficiently understand what marriage is and its essential properties." [15] Similarly Cappello states that those contracting marriage must know the conjugal rights and duties. Wherefore the mere use of reason is not enough, but a sufficient maturity of judgment and discretion is required so that what pertains to the essence of marriage be known to the spouses.[16]

Precisely what must be known about marriage before proper consent can be given is reasonably affirmed by Payen: [17]

> " It is necessary that both contracting parties know three things about the marriage state, in the first place, that it is a permanent society, not entered for a brief time, nor dissoluble at will; secondly, that it is a society established between persons of different sexes; thirdly, and especially, that it is a society which pertains to the procreation of children, and not to another primary end. These three are essential."

These essential elements of marriage do not contain any reference to age. It does not seem to be an unwarranted conclusion that by natural law no specified age is required as a condition for validly entering a marriage. Whenever the necessary use of reason and the sufficient maturity of judgment and discretion is reached, at that point a valid marriage, by natural law, may be contracted. Age in itself, that is, the actual number of years, is not an essential factor of marriage. However, age at some given point does serve to indicate that the person possesses the required

---

[15] Gasparri, *loc. cit.* Writer's translation.

[16] *De Sacramentis,* III, n. 581.

[17] *De Matrimonio, in Missionibus et Potissimum in Sinis Tractatus Practicus et Casus* (2. ed., 3 vols., Zi-ka-wei: In typographia T'ou-sè-wè, 1935–1936), II, n. 1623 (hereafter cited as *De Matrimonio*). Writer's translation.

knowledge to give proper consent. It may set up a presumption because a normal person at a certain age ordinarily has acquired sufficient knowledge and is capable of expressing free consent. But the point to be emphasized is that the natural capacity to give consent is of the essence of marriage and natural law does not prescribe any determined age before the attaining of which it cannot be given. On this point there is unanimity among the canonical authorities.[18]

It follows as a consequent, then, that when the Church by her law forbids any one of her male subjects from entering marriage before the completion of the specifically determined sixteenth year, or any female before the completion of her fourteenth year, the Church is adding a requirement that is over and above the natural law. Moreover, the very fact that the Church has altered her law and has increased the age necessary for marriage is evidence that the present law is not an exact specification of the natural law. Such considerations make clear the conclusion that the impediment of nonage is of positive and merely ecclesiastical law.

ARTICLE 2: *Requisite Physical Capacity*

While stressing mental capacity, that is, consent, as an essential prerequisite to marriage, especially in its relation to age, the physical capacity cannot be ignored. It may be reasonably asked: does not the natural law demand that persons attain the age of puberty before they can validly contract marriage? In the light of the object of marriage and its primary end, namely the procreation and the education of children,[19] it might seem that sexual maturity to fulfill that purpose of marriage is required by nature

[18] Schmalzgrueber, *Ius Ecclesiasticum Universum* (5 vols. in 12, Romae, 1843–1845), lib. IV, tit. II, n. 48; Reiffenstuel, *Ius Canonicum Universum* (5 vols. in 7, Parisiis, 1864–1870), lib. IV, tit. II, n. 10; Wernz, *Ius Matrimoniale,* n. 319; Cappello, *De Sacramentis,* III, n. 336; Ayrinac-Lydon, *Marriage Legislation in the New Code of Canon Law,* p. 124; Payen, *De Matrimonio,* I, n. 953.

[19] Canon 1013, § 1. Matrimonium finis primarius est procreatio atque educatio prolis; secundarius mutuum adiutorium et remedium concupiscentiae.

itself. However, by means of a further analysis of the true nature of marriage, it can be shown that puberty is not a requirement for marriage on the part of the natural law.

The law of the Code in determining the minimum age for marriage at sixteen for boys and fourteen for girls has severed the direct relationship between the age of marriage and the age of puberty which was the basis for the pre-Code law. But the Code still retains the legal presumption that a boy attains puberty at the age of fourteen and the girl at the age of twelve.[20] Likewise it presumes that those who have attained puberty are not ignorant of the essential features of marriage and are capable of giving a true matrimonial consent.[21]

By puberty is meant the initial stage of adolescence, the earliest age at which the individual is capable of begetting offspring.[22] It is that period of life at which a person of either sex becomes functionally capable of generation.[23] For boys the attainment of factual puberty is physiologically computed, to quote Antonelli, "*a tempore quo testes conficiunt sperma.*" [24] Externally the attainment of this period of development can be recognized by the greater size of the organs of generation, by the appearance of the pubic hair, by the growth of a beard, and by the changing of the voice.[25] At what age this development takes place cannot be exactly determined, for it varies in the individual boy and is influenced by such factors as general health, social condition, place of habitation,

---

[20] Canon 88, § 1. Persona quae vicesimum primum aetatis annum explevit, maior est; infra hanc aetatem, minor. §2. Minor, si masculus, censetur pubes a decimoquarto, si femina a duodecimo anno completo.

[21] Canon 1082, § 1. Ut matrimonialis consensus haberi possit, necesse est ut contrahentes saltem non ignorent matrimonium esse societatem permanentem inter virum et mulierem ad filios procreandos. §2. Haec ignorantia post pubertatem non praesumitur.

[22] Brooks, *The Psychology of Adolescence* (Boston: Houghton Mifflin Co., 1929), p. 1.

[23] Schumacher, *The Adolescent, His Development and His Major Problem* (Washington, D. C.: The Catholic Conference on Family Life, 1938), p. 2.

[24] *Medicina Pastoralis in Usum Confessorum et Curiarum Ecclesiasticarum* (3. ed., 3 vols., Romae, 1909), I, 188 (hereafter cited *Medicina Pastoralis*).

[25] Antonelli, *loc. cit.*

climate, all of which are factors which may accelerate or retard it. But ordinarily it will take place between the ages of thirteen and sixteen.[26] This stage of sexual maturity is reached by the American boy at the average proximate age of fourteen and a half or fifteen years.[27] It must be noted, however, that while with puberty the boy is capable of the act of generation, yet, to quote Eschbach: "sperum conficere tunc incipit, sed usque dum decimum circiter sextum aut septimum annum attingat, istud non prolificum, seu spermatizoidis refertum." [28] Ordinarily there is a natural sterility until the boy reaches the age of sixteen or seventeen.

For girls the attainment of puberty is at an earlier age and it is usually indicated by the first menstruation. Schumacher notes [29] that it is not correct to say that puberty in girls always begins with the first menstruation period, for it has been shown that the menstrual cycle may be initiated before ovulation begins. However, ordinarily menstruation is the sign. Other indications are the appearance of pubic hair and the enlargement of the breasts.[30] As in the case of boys, the age at which this stage of development is attained is variable, but generally considered, the hotter the climate, the earlier the girls will mature and the shorter will be the whole period for the perfection of their maturity.[31] There is evidence that the Indians in the plains of Peru mature at the age of nine,[32] while in northern countries, such as Norway, rarely does this development take place before the age of sixteen or seventeen.[33] The median chronological age for American girls is approximately thirteen and a half to thirteen and three-quarter years.[34]

---

[26] Antonelli, *loc. cit.*

[27] Brooks, *op. cit.*, p. 43.

[28] Eschbach, *Disputationes Physiologico-Theologicae* (Romae: Declée, Lefebure et Socii, 1901), p. 35.

[29] *Op. cit.*, p. 10.

[30] Antonelli, *op. cit.*, I, n. 205.

[31] Richmond-Hall, *Child Marriages* (New York: Russell Sage Foundation, 1925), p. 30.

[32] *Loc. cit.*

[33] Antonelli, *loc. cit.*

[34] Brooks, *op. cit.*, p. 42.

The arrival at puberty, however, and the actual attainment of the physical capacity to perform the marriage act which is associated with puberty is not required by the natural law before a valid marriage can be contracted. The fact that a person has not yet attained to puberty will obviously prevent him or her from the use of marriage, because he is physically inept and unprepared for that use. But marriage does not essentially consist in its use, rather in the consent to and transference of the right to the use of marriage. This point can be stated with certainty, for basically it is the accepted canonical teaching of Canon 1081, § 1, which declares that the consent of the parties makes the marriage. To say that the use of marriage is involved in or necessary for marriage is to accept the discarded and refuted "*copula*" theory, which wrongly maintained that the consummation or the use of marriage was necessary for its completion and perfection.[35]

Even though one who is still in the state of impuberty does not yet have the physical potency for the use of marriage, which is the object of the marriage contract, nevertheless because in due time, in the course of natural growth and development, he will have that potency, he can presently transfer the right. The present and temporary inability to use the right does not prevent or hinder its present transference. It is the transference and acceptance of the right that is of the essence of marriage.

It is in this regard that impuberty must be distinguished from impotence as an impediment to marriage. It is only a certain, antecedent and perpetual impotence which by the very law of nature impedes marriage.[36] While impuberty is impotence, it is not permanent. One who is perpetually impotent can never place the act which is in and of itself fitted for the generation of chil-

[35] For a lengthier discussion of the "*copula*" theory consult: Dillon, *Common Law Marriage* (The Catholic University of America Canon Law Studies, n. 170, Washington, D. C.: The Catholic University of America Press, 1942), pp. 26–31; Joyce, *Christian Marriage*, pp. 56–51; De Smet, *Tractatus Theologico-Canonicus De Sponsalibus et Matrimonio* (ed. quarta inde a Codice altera, Brugis: Car. Beyaert, 1927), nn. 96–99 (hereafter cited *De Sponsalibus et Matrimonio*).

[36] Canon 1068, § 1. Impotentia antecedens et perpetua, sive ex parte viri, sive ex parte mulieris, sive alteri cognita, sive non, sive absoluta, sive relativa, matrimonium ipso naturae iure dirimit.

dren. Hence he or she is not capable of making the contract of marriage which has as its object the use of a right which he or she will never possess. The very material of the matrimonial contract is lacking, so the contract, lacking an object, is null.[37] But the one who is still in the state of impuberty will have the power or potency to fulfill the object of the contract and therefore can transfer that right. The object of the contract is possible, not immediately, but certainly in the future. It is sufficient for a contract, by the natural law, that the material of the contract exist as a thing which can be expected to become operative and to be realized only later.[38]

That puberty is not required by natural law for a valid marriage has been clearly manifested by varied responses of the Holy See. The Vicar Apostolic of Hunan, China, asked the Holy Office whether those children who, according to the Chinese custom, were married while still in infidelity, could cohabit, if they were converted with their whole family. The response was to the effect that Christian *impuberes,* who had contracted marriage while still pagans, must be separated and could not live together, unless the condition of "*malitia supplet aetatem*" was present, but that they had the obligation of living together matrimonially when they arrived at the age of puberty, provided that the marriage was not proved null by some impediment of the natural or divine law, or particularly because of lack of consent.[39]

Not many years after this response the Holy Office was asked in another case whether spouses who were married before the attainment of puberty while pagans and without any consummation of the marriage could be considered as having contracted only "*sponsalia de futuro,*" and not a real marriage, if one of the spouses was converted to the faith. The response from the Holy Office was that as long as it was clear that there was no impediment of the natural or positive divine law, and especially that the contracting parties gave true consent, such contracts were not *sponsalia* but true marriages.[40]

---

[37] Cappello, *De Sacramentis,* III, n. 347.

[38] Tanquerey, *Synopsis Theologicae Moralis et Pastoralis,* III, n. 619, b.

[39] S.C.S. Off. (Hu-nan), 2 maii 1866, ad 2—*Collectanea SCPF,* n. 1289.

[40] S.C.S. Off., 10 dec. 1885—*Fontes,* n. 1097; *Collectanea SCPF,* n. 1645.

It is thus evident both from intrinsic and extrinsic arguments that puberty is not postulated by the natural law for a valid marriage. Similarly if a boy who is subject to the Church's law on the impediment of nonage has completed his sixteenth year, or a girl her fourteenth year, yet by way of exception neither has yet attained puberty actually, nevertheless they could still contract a valid marriage. Legally the boy is presumed to have arrived at puberty at the age of fourteen, and the girl at the age of twelve, but if *de facto* that development has been retarded and has not yet been reached at the completion of the sixteenth year for the boy, or the fourteenth year for the girl, notwithstanding this and on the ground of the requisite age they are free to marry. It is true of course that this point did have wider application under the pre-Code law than under the present legislation. But the possibility of such a case still exists.

To the point is a case judged by the Sacred Congregation of the Council on February 6, 1847.[41] A boy had contracted marriage while still physically *impubes,* though in actual years he was two months over the legal age of fourteen. The diocesan court (Angra in Portugal) had declared the marriage null by reason of the impediment of nonage on the grounds that actual potency as well as the legitimate age was required for a valid marriage. But the Sacred Congregation overruled this sentence and criticized the legal reasoning of the diocesan curia, declaring that the impediment of nonage did not nullify the marriage, for the impediment ceased either by completion of the determined number of years, or by the actual attainment of puberty. If the age had been attained prior to the marriage, actual potency was not then a consideration.

---

[41] S.C.C., Angren., 6 febr. 1847—*Thesaurus Resolutionum Sacrae Congregationis Concilii* (167 vols., Romae, 1718–1908), CVII, 59 (hereafter cited *Thesaurus Resolutionum S.C.C.*); Pallottini, *Collectio omnium Conclusionum et Resolutionum quae in causis propositis apud Sacram Congregationem, Cardinalium S. Concilii Tridentini interpretum Prodierunt ab eius institutione anno MDLXIV ad MDCCCLX, distinctis titulis alphabetico ordine per materias digestas* (18 vols., Romae, 1868–1893), s.v. *Matrimonium Quoad Impedimentum Dirimens Aetatis,* XII, 533 (hereafter cited as Pallottini, *Collectio*).

But whether or not those who have completed the necessary age for marriage, yet are still physiologically *impuberes,* can licitly marry is a question which is treated by Payen. If they enter marriage with the intention of postponing their common life until both parties have attained puberty physiologically and have become capable of the use of marriage, he maintains that it is clear that such a marriage would be licit.[42] But if they intend to cohabit immediately and use marriage, such a marriage would be inherently illicit because of the grave danger of sin. However, he remarks also that rarely would such a marriage be subjectively illicit because before marriage those contracting the marriage would rarely know with certainty that they were not capable of properly performing the marriage act.[43]

Such questions, however, seem rather remote and rather of a speculative than of a practical nature, especially in view of the obligation imposed on the pastor of dissuading from marriage those who are below the age customary in a particular region.[44] The problem could have arisen more readily under the pre-Code law when the legal age of marriage was fourteen for boys and twelve for girls. Then the possibility of the parties completing the necessary age and still not yet possessing the *potestas generandi et carnaliter coeundi* was more likely to occur. So it was that the pre-Code authors gave some consideration to the problem.[45] However, the point serves to emphasize the fact that puberty is not required by the natural law or by the ecclesiastical law for the validity of a marriage.

ARTICLE 3: *Reasonableness of the Impediment of Nonage*

It has been insisted in the foregoing pages that the natural law does not specify any definite impediment of nonage, and that its

[42] Payen, *De Matrimonio,* I, n. 949.

[43] *Loc. cit.*

[44] Canon 1067, §2.

[45] Sanchez, *De Matrimonio,* lib. VII, disp. 104, n .15; Pirhing, *Ius Canonicum in Quinque Libros Decretalium Distributum Nova Methodo Explicatum* (ed. novissima, 5 vols. in 4, Dilingae, 1722), lib. IV, tit. II, n. 7; Reiffenstuel, *Ius Canonicum Universum,* lib. IV, tit. II, n. 7; Schmalzgrueber, *Ius Ecclesiasticum Universum,* lib. IV, tit. II, n. 51; Wernz, *Ius Matrimoniale,* n. 321.

sole demand in regard to the age at which marriage may be contracted is that the person have the necessary mental maturity to give true matrimonial consent. This very lack of the determination by the natural law of an impediment of nonage is the basis on which rests the reasonableness of the act of competent authority in specifying and determining such an impediment. Natural law is content to manifest its claims in broad outline, to postulate general principles.

It is a right and within the competence of legitimately constituted authority by its positive law to add further requirements for the good of individuals and of society provided that these additions do not go contrary to the natural law.[46] It is for the good of society and for the individuals involved to prevent and forbid marriage until its purpose can be fulfilled. As Reiffenstuel (1641–1703) remarked, it is reasonable and just to forbid marriage until its primary end can be fulfilled, that is, until the *potestas generandi et carnaliter coeundi* is attained.[47]

It was simply this that the pre-Code impediment of nonage aimed at accomplishing. However, to allow marriage, or not to forbid it, when the boy or girl had arrived at the minimum age of physical capacity was not a sufficient safeguard to their own physical and moral health, nor did it provide a reasonable assurance for the well-being of the offspring of such a youthful marriage. It has been stated that above the age of puberty child-bearing is possible, but biologically the bearing of children is detrimental, or at least disadvantageous, until the bodily frame of the mother has had time to store up a reserve of vigor which was scarcely attainable during the period of its rapid growth and quick development.[48] Antonelli adds further confirmation to this claim.[49] There are many reasons, hygienic, moral and social,

---

[46] Cf. Gasparri, *De Matrimonio,* I, n. 250.

[47] *Ius Ecclesiasticum Universum,* lib. IV, tit. II, n. 6.

[48] Richmond-Hall, *Child Marriage,* p. 25.

[49] *Medicina Pastoralis,* II, 729: "Quoad alterum elementum [corpus physice bene evolutum] physiologice considerandum, ut ex matrimonio optimi effectus consequantur, evidens est corpus coniugum debere esse plene evolutum, robustum, physice sanum, adeo ut possint fortem ac sanam prolem gignere."

which urge that those not sufficiently mature be prevented from marriage. When the new Code of canon law was in the preparatory stage Wernz (1842–1914) proposed the following reasons for a change in the existing law on the impediment of nonage: [50]

"1. The principal purpose of marriage is the conservation of the human race; now, if marriages are contracted too early, degeneration of the race occurs, as experience proves. 2. It is of great importance that the law take care of public morality; now, public morality loses considerably if marriages are permitted at too early an age, as are the ages of fourteen and twelve for boys and girls respectively, because these marriages, like others, postulate a time of preparation for them, and girls enter courtship at an age in which they should in no way think of marriage. 3. Civil laws have increased the requirement regarding the necessary age for marriage, and thus in all civilized countries it would create a strange impression to see a marriage contracted at the age of twelve and fourteen; now, in reality, law should be adapted to customs. Indeed, the missionaries themselves, for example in India, see the difficulties and the grave consequences, even physical ones, of marriages contracted at too early an age, and insist that the girls should at least have arrived at the age of thirteen or fourteen."

If the minimum ages of sixteen–fourteen established by the Code seem to be an inadequate minimum to protect and safeguard the individual and social well-being, it must be borne in mind that the law of the Code must be such as to be universally applicable to all who are to be subject to that law. It embraces not only those who live in the temperate zone, but also those who live in the torrid zone, where maturity is attained at an early age and where physical development is more rapid. Moreover, it is neither the purpose nor the intent of the impediment to set up a standard age for marriage. The impediment establishes a minimum age below which marriage cannot be validly contracted, but it does not determine a norm to regulate the age at which marriage should be contracted. Sufficient cognizance of local condi-

[50] Gasparri, *De Matrimonio,* I, p. 292, nota 1. Writer's translation.

tions and practice has been taken by the second paragraph of canon 1067, in which the obligation is imposed on pastors to dissuade from marriage those who would contract it below an age which the wisdom deriving from the observation of particular circumstances dictates.

CHAPTER III

Those Subject to the Ecclesiastical Impediment *of* Nonage

It has been indicated and demonstrated that the impediment of nonage as expressed by canon 1067, § 1, is an ecclesiastical impediment. The Church, employing the competence that is hers, has enacted a disqualifying law, that is, a law which renders a person juridically incapable of placing a determined act which of itself and in consideration only of the divine law, natural or positive, would be valid.[1] Hence the impediment has the force and value of an ecclesiastical law, which means that it is binding only on those who are subject to and bound by the law of the Code. It becomes necessary, then, to classify more exactly those who in contracting marriage are under this merely ecclesiastical law and those who are free from its effects.

Article 1: *Those Bound by the Impediment of Nonage*

In canon 12 the general principle is stated that those who have not received baptism are not bound by merely ecclesiastical laws. Similarly canon 87 in a positive manner indicates that by baptism a man is constituted a person in the Church of Christ with all the concomitant rights and duties. By divine law itself only those who have been validly baptized are members of the Church of Christ on earth and subject to its laws. This is true because baptism is the door by which one enters the House of God, the Church.[2] No one is bound by the laws of any society unless he is

[1] Beste, *Introductio in Codicem* (Collegeville, Minnesota: St. John's Abbey Press, 1938), p. 66.

[2] McCloskey, *The Subject of Ecclesiastical Law According to Canon 12,* The Catholic University of America Canon Law Studies, n. 165 (Washington, D. C.: The Catholic University of America Press, 1943), p. 77.

a member of that society. But it is only through the baptism of water validly received that a man becomes a member of the Church.[3] More specifically in relation to marriage, canon 1016 states that the marriage of the baptized is regulated not only by the divine law, but also by canon law.

It is not only baptized Catholics who are considered within the scope of these general principles, but all those who are validly baptized, including heretics, apostates and schismatics. As McCloskey remarks: [4]

> ". . . in the Church which is a perfect society the external ceremony that creates this bond of union is Baptism. But because of the peculiar effect of valid Baptism, namely, the imprinting of an indelible character or mark on the human soul, the bond of union with the Church takes on a special quality of permanence. Hence, this union can never be broken. Even though a baptized person may cease to be a *member* of the Church by separating himself from the number of the faithful, juridically he will still be *subject* to the Church's jurisdiction. Also those persons who are validly baptized outside of the Church and never are *members* of the Church, are juridically subject to the jurisdiction of the Church because of the indelible mark of baptism, which every valid baptism imprints on the soul. This same effect occurs whether the valid baptism is administered in the Catholic Church or in an heretical sect."

All those, then, who are validly baptized are subject to the law of the Church, unless they are specifically or expressly exempted by the Church from that law. There is an abundance of evidence that it is not the mind of the Church that baptized heretics, schismatics or apostates be excluded from its matrimonial legislation. In the Code itself in those canons in which a general reference is made to the right of the Church in matrimonial matters, no distinction is to be found between baptized Catholics

---

[3] Beste, *Introductio in Codicem,* p. 68.

[4] *Op. cit.,* pp. 108–109.

and baptized non-Catholics,[5] but the term "*baptizatis,*" or its equivalent, is used without any qualification or restriction.

By the general norms of interpretation ecclesiastical laws must be understood according to the proper meaning of the words in the text and context.[6] There would be no justification whatsoever for interpreting "the baptized" to mean simply baptized Catholics. Furthermore, Gasparri (1852–1936) remarks that in the preparation of the Code it was proposed to the consultors that a general principle be included in the Code to the effect that only those who were baptized in the Catholic Church be bound by the ecclesiastical laws on marriage. But this principle did not meet with their approval.[7] This decision clearly indicates the mind of those who framed the Code. However, the Code does expressly exempt baptized non-Catholics from the impediment of disparity of cult,[8] and from the prescribed canonical form of marriage,[9] which facts point to the conclusion that baptized non-Catholics are bound to the other impediments which the Code has enacted.[10]

Of the papal documents and responses that bear out the general principle that the baptized non-Catholics are bound by the canonical impediments,[11] there is one in particular that clearly demonstrates that it is the mind of the Holy See that baptized Protestants are bound by the canonical impediment of nonage. The case was submitted from Pondichery, India, where it happened that

---

[5] Canons 1016; 1038, § 2; 1960.

[6] Canon 18.

[7] Gasparri, *De Matrimonio,* I, n. 257, nota 2.

[8] Canon 1070, § 1.

[9] Canon 1099, § 2.

[10] Cf. Vermeersch-Creusen, *Epitome Iuris Canonici* (3 vols., Vol. I, ed. sexta, 1937, Vol. II, ed. quinta, 1936, Vol. III, ed. quinta, 1936, Mechlinae-Romae: H. Dessain), I, n. 106 (hereafter cited *Epitome*); Cappello, *De Sacramentis,* III, n. 66; Gasparri, *De Matrimonio,* I, n. 257; Payen, *De Matrimonio,* I, n. 196.

[11] Benedictus XIV, ep. encycl., "*Singulari nobis,*" 9 febr. 1749—*Fontes,* n. 394; Benedictus XIV, ep. encycl., "*Magnae Nobis,*" 29 iun. 1749—*Fontes,* n. 387; S.C.S. Off., instr. (ad Vic. Ap. Gallas), 28 mart. 1860—*Fontes,* n. 957; S.C.C., *Rosnavien,* 20 aug. 1780—*Fontes,* n. 3811.

a Protestant girl was married at the age of eleven. After she lived with her husband for some time, he deserted her. By the law of India, after a period of seven years has elapsed the missing spouse is presumed to be dead. After that period of time had passed the woman desired to marry a Catholic. The priest refused to witness the marriage, and the couple went before a minister. The priest then submitted the case to the Holy Office and asked whether the first marriage of the woman could be considered invalid on the grounds of lack of age. The Holy Office responded that the invalidity would be most difficult to prove, but it could be if it seemed morally certain to the Vicar Apostolic that the acts of the trial proved that the woman was married before she completed her twelfth year, that at that time the condition of "*malitia supplet aetatem*" was not fulfilled, and finally that after attaining puberty she did not have marriage relations with the man. If these facts were demonstrated and proved, then the first marriage could be declared null on the grounds of the impediment of nonage.[12] It was the law of the Church in force at that time that was to be applied. Hence baptized non-Catholics were bound by the impediment of nonage.

With reference solely to the item of age, no baptized non-Catholic boy or girl can validly contract marriage below the age prescribed by the ecclesiastical law which constitutes the impediment. If they attempt marriage before the canonical age, their marriage is invalid. It may also be mentioned at this point that since the impediment is in effect a disqualifying law, neither ignorance nor good faith frees anyone from the obligation of the law, to which the person is subject.[13] While such a marriage would be invalid, even if there was good faith on the part of either or both parties, it would still be a putative marriage.[14]

[12] S.C.S. Off. (Pondichery), 28 iun. 1865—*Fontes,* n. 984; *Collectanea SCPF,* n. 1273.

[13] Canon 16, § 1. Nulla ignorantia legum irritantium aut inhabilitantium ab eisdem excusat, nisi aliud expresse dicatur.

[14] Canon 1015, § 4. Matrimonium invalidum dicitur *putativum,* si in bona fide ab una saltem parte celebratum fuerit, donec utraque pars de eiusdem nullitate certa evadat.

Article 2: *Those Not Bound by the Canonical Impediment of Nonage*

A. The Unbaptized

1. The Unbaptized Are Not Bound by the Ecclesiastical Law

It is the clear and undisputed principle of canon 12 that those who have not been baptized are also not bound by merely ecclesiastical laws. Since the impediment of nonage comes within the category of merely ecclesiastical laws, it follows that those who have not been baptized are not subject to this impediment. So infidels and catechumens are not limited or restricted by this impediment when contracting marriage. It hardly seems necessary to belabor this intrinsic argument.[15]

Extrinsically, on the authority of the Holy See, there have been responses which directly indicate that infidels are not bound by the impediment of nonage. In 1734 Pope Clement XII (1736–1740) in an apostolic letter to the missionaries of India and the Orient gave an answer to proposed doubts. It was the custom in those regions for children of six or seven years of age, with the consent of their parents, to contract indissoluble marriage. As a sign that it was a real marriage, the girl wore a golden pendant (tally). The missionaries were ordered in this apostolic letter not to allow such marriage, since they were null among Christians. If Christians did attempt such marriages they were not to be allowed to cohabit until they had completed the legitimate and canonical age and thereupon had also given their free consent according to the form prescribed by the Council of Trent.[16]

---

[15] Cf. Cappello, *De Sacramentis,* III, n. 67; Wernz-Vidal, *Ius Matrimoniale* (2. ed., 1928—Vol. V of *Ius Canonicum,* 7 vols. in 8, Romae: apud Aedes Universitas Gregorianae, 1923–1938), n. 57; Coronata, *Institutiones Iuris Canonici* (5 vols., Taurini: Marietti, Vol. III, 1933; Vol. IV, 1935; Vol. V, 1936; Vols. I–II, 1939), I, n. 14.

[16] Clemens XII, lit. ap., "*Compertum,*" 24 aug. 1734, dubium V, n. 40—*Fontes,* n. 296. The substance of this same letter was again stressed by Pope Clement XII (lit. ap., "*Concredita Nobis,*" 13 maii 1739—*Fontes* n. 300) together with the declaration that an obligation was imposed on the missionaries of taking an oath to fulfill it; it was again repeated by Pope

The specific statement that such marriages were *null for Christians* seems to carry the implication that they could be valid for infidels, or, in other words, that the impediment of nonage did not bind the infidels. But to preclude the necessity of deducing this principle as a conclusion from these papal letters, the two responses from the Holy Office already referred to [17] clearly declared that infidels could contract a valid marriage even before they attained to the age of puberty, and hence were not bound by the impediment of nonage.[18]

2. The Unbaptized Are Bound by the Civil Impediment of Nonage

But the unbaptized in contracting marriage among themselves are bound by any reasonable and just impediment of nonage, whether diriment or impeding, which the competent civil authority to which they are subject may establish.[19] While it must be admitted that the right of the state to establish diriment impediments to marriage for the unbaptized has been called into question, nevertheless neither the weight of the arguments proposed nor the weight of the authors who propose them seems to have been able to compel an incontestable admission of the claim that the state is deprived of that right. The earlier canonists and theologians were in common agreement, and taught as certain that the civil authority could legislate for the natural contract of marriage among the unbaptized, just as it could for any other contract.[20]

However, in a theory first advanced by Jean Pey (1740–1797) in the year 1788,[21] and subsequently defended among others by

---

Benedict XIV (const., "*Omnium sollicitudinum,*" 12 sept. 1744, dubium V, n. 14—*Fontes,* n. 348).

[17] Cf. *supra,* p. 22.

[18] S.C.S. Off. (Hu-nan), 2 maii, 1866—*Collectamea SCPF,* n. 1289; S.C.S. Off., 10 dec. 1885—*Fontes,* n. 1097; *Collectanea SCPF* n. 1645.

[19] Wernz-Vidal, *Ius Matrimoniale,* n. 211.

[20] E.g., Schmalzgrueber, *Ius Ecclesiasticum Universum,* lib. IV, tit. I, n. 364; Sanchez, *De Matrimonio,* lib. VIII, disp. 3, n. 5; cf. Wernz-Vidal, *Ius Matrimoniale,* n. 68, and Dillon, *Common Law Marriage,* p. 64, for the mention and citation of additional authors.

[21] *De l'autorité des deux puissances* (4 vols., Strasbourg, 1788), III, p. 158 ss.; Wernz-Vidal, *op. cit.,* n. 68; Dillon, *op. cit.,* p. 65.

Liberatore (1810–1892),[22] Perrone (1794–1876) [23] and Feije (1820–1894),[24] it was maintained that the civil authority had no competence to establish diriment impediments which would make its unbaptized subjects incapable of contracting marriage. The theory rested on three intrinsic arguments, as Dillon points out: [25] "(1) Marriage is by its nature something sacred, so that it cannot come under the competency of mere civil society; (2) civil authority cannot legislate for an internal act, such as is necessary to constitute a true bond of marriage; (3) marriage pertains to the law of nature, and therefore not to civil law."

As Gasparri remarks,[26] if these arguments are drawn to their logical conclusion, not only would the state's right to establish diriment impediments for the marriages of the unbaptized be excluded, but also its right to establish impeding impediments as well, as even the Church's right to institute impediments. Neither of these points would or could the proponents of this theory attempt to maintain.

But the arguments themselves do not have validity in proving the desired point. In the first place, that marriage has by its nature a sanctity even for the unbaptized will be granted, but that the civil authority has not competency over sacred things cannot be accepted. The very fact that the unbaptized are not direct subjects of the Church makes it necessary that there be some authority to determine and regulate even sacred things for them. There are only two perfect societies in the world, the Church and the State.[27] The incompetency of the Church forces the conclusion that the civil authority must be competent for the

---

[22] *Institutiones Philosophicae,* Vol. III, *Ethica et Ius Naturae* (8. ed., Romae, 1885), lib. II, chap. 1, art. 4.

[23] *De Matrimonio Christiano* (3 vols., Romae, 1858) II, 439–470.

[24] *De Impedimentis et Dispensationibus Matrimonialibus,* n. 67–70. This author admitted that the opinion of those acknowledging this power to the state was the more common one, but maintained that it was not supported by arguments which had sufficient validity to cause him to relinquish the opposite opinion.

[25] *Op. cit.,* p. 66.

[26] *Op. cit.,* I, n. 248.

[27] Ottaviani, *Institutiones Iuris Publici Ecclesiastici* (ed. altera, 2 vols., Civitate Vaticana: Typis Polyglottis Vaticanis, 1935–1936), I, 64.

unbaptized, otherwise very necessary relations in society would fail to have a proper supervision and regulation.[28]

The fact that marriage is under the natural law does not militate against the right of the state to legislate for its unbaptized subjects any more than that fact does not deprive the Church of her competency for the baptized. Certainly no human authority, whether civil or ecclesiastical, can make laws that are contrary to the natural law, but to complement with precise prescriptions and prohibitions, to clarify and further specify the natural law for the good of the community, clearly does not encroach upon or interfere with the law of nature.[29]

As for the final intrinsic argument against the right of the state to establish diriment impediments, namely, that marriage is anterior to the civil government and therefore cannot be regulated by it, it bears out the contention of Gasparri that all the arguments of the opposition are based on abstract principles which lose their value as arguments as soon as the necessary distinctions are properly invoked and applied.[30] Logically marriage is the very foundation of the state, but once the state has been established, it exists ahead of subsequent marriage. To protect itself, to safeguard the interests of the community, and to secure the common good, the civil authority can and, so it appears, must regulate the subsequent marriages of its unbaptized subjects for the common well-being.

But proof of the competency of the civil authority to establish diriment impediments for its unbaptized subjects does not rest solely on intrinsic arguments, nor on the apparent invalidity of the arguments advanced by the advocates of the contrary opinion. There are also extrinsic arguments in the form of responses which express the practical mind of the Holy See. While it must be admitted, as Ayrinhac-Lydon point out, [31] that there has been no general and final decision of the Holy See in this matter, nevertheless the particular responses of the Sacred Congregations

---

[28] Dillon, *op. cit.*, pp. 67–68; Gasparri, *op. cit.*, I, n. 249.

[29] Cf. Gasparri, *op. cit.*, n. 250; Dillon, *op. cit.*, p. 70.

[30] Gasparri, *op. cit.*, I, n. 248.

[31] *Marriage Legislation in the New Code of Canon Law*, p. 13.

furnish sufficient certitude for a basis of action and offer a practical solution for the problem.

At a general session of the Sacred Congregation of the Propagation of the Faith on December 5, 1631, presided over by Cardinal Pamphylius, an instruction was sent to the missionaries of India, not, however, as a decree of the Congregation, but as the opinion of theologians and canonists. The instruction contained the following: " Polygamists of India, who together with all their wives, become converted to the Faith and receive baptism, must dismiss all their wives except their first, who is the real wife, if in her marriage there was no impediment of the natural law or of the positive law established by their civil leader.[32] The expressed condition of the instruction, even though it was insisted by the Congregation that it be regarded as the opinion of canonists, and not as its own formal decree, argues for the competency of the civil authority to establish diriment impediments for the unbaptized.

Even more directly does another response from this same Congregation solve the question. A case was submitted by the Vicar Apostolic of Tunking, China: " An unbaptized man, who had entered marriage with an unbaptized woman, having omitted certain ceremonies the omission of which was considered a diriment impediment to marriage according to the laws of Tunking, left this woman and took to wife another who was a Christian; he himself, embracing the Christian faith, then sought baptism. Was he held to interpellate his first wife, whom he had deserted, as to whether or not she desired to become a Christian, and wished to return to live with him, or at least to cohabit with him peaceably and without contempt of God? If his first wife became a Christian, or at least agreed to live peaceably with him, was he bound to go back to her? If he became reconciled with his first wife and there was a true legitimate marriage between them, were they to renew their matrimonial consent? To put it briefly, did a diriment impediment which was established by an unbaptized legislator, or accepted through long-standing custom, render marriages

[32] *Collectanea SCPF,* n. 1308.

void and invalid between unbaptized men and women contracted with such an impediment?"

On June 26, 1820, the Sacred Congregation of Propagation of the Faith responded: "Both the first and the second marriages are null; there is no need for interpellations, but with the proper observance of all the requisites there was an occasion for a new marriage and let an instruction be given." [33] In the footnote of the *Collectanea,*[34] the instruction referred to in the response is given, and it states the principle that marriage among the unbaptized is governed by the natural and civil law, and hence the civil rulers, whether Christian or pagan, possess a plenitude of power over the marriages of their unbaptized subjects and can establish impediments which effectively invalidate marriage.[35]

But whether or not this Instruction received the approval of the Sacred Congregation seems to be a question. Gasparri [36] is content to say that it probably did, but that it is not certain. However, as Wernz-Vidal [37] point out, the response itself is sufficient proof of the point, for the Congregation could not rule on the particular case and declare the marriages null together with asserting the right to the parties to enter a new marriage unless there was certain proof both in law and in fact of the nullity of the previous marriages. The whole question in the proposed case was the efficacy of the civil law impediment. The

[33] *Collectanea SCPF,* n. 744. Writer's translation.

[34] *Ibid.,* nota 1.

[35] ". . . Quare licet inter infideles verum sit matrimonium, tamen ad naturae et communitatis officium referri tantummodo potest, ac proinde a iure naturae ac civili plane est moderandum. Sequitur hinc Principes saeculares sive fideles sive infideles plenissimam potestatem retinere in matrimoniis subditorum infidelium; ut scilicet appositis impedimentis quae iuri naturali ac divino adversa non sint, eadem non solum quoad civiles effectus, sed etiam quoad coniugale vinculum penitus rescindant. Qui enim, ob Reipublicae bonum, suis legibus ad legitimitatem validitatemque ceterorum contractuum formam quamdam, et solemnitatibus praescribere possunt, cur id in matrimoniali infidelium subditorum contractu efficere nequeant, ratio non est; et quod de lege Principis saecularis hoc in casu dicitur, intellige etiam de legitima consuetudine, quae vim legis in subditos infideles adepta est."—*Loc. cit.*

[36] *De Matrimonio,* I, n. 247.

[37] *Ius Matrimoniale,* n. 72, nota 78.

practical decision, i.e. a declaration of the nullity of the marriage with the indication of full liberty to enter another marriage is not given, nor can be given, without certain proof of law and fact, otherwise the divine law concerning the impediment of *ligamen* would be most gravely violated.[38]

It can be said, then, with Doheny: [39] "If the civil law of a particular state or country contains a diriment impediment of age, the marriage of two infidels under age would be void in the eyes of the state and consequently would be similarly viewed by the Church." But whether or not the civil law intends to make the impediment of nonage a diriment or an impeding impediment is a question of fact which must be solved in each jurisdiction by means of an investigation of the civil law in force in that locality.[40] In the last chapter of this treatise will be listed the effect of the law in the various States of the United States.

3. Marriage Between an Unbaptized Person Civilly Impeded and a Baptized Person

When two unbaptized persons intermarry there seems to be no doubt that they are bound by any reasonable and just impediment of nonage established by the competent civil authority to which they are subject. However, a problem arises when an unbaptized person, who is still below the age determined by the civil authority for entering a valid marriage, wishes to marry a Catholic, who by all canonical norms is free to marry. Provided, of course, that a dispensation from the impediment of disparity of cult would have been obtained, would the civil impediment of nonage bind the unbaptized party and make him or her incapable of marriage with the canonically free Catholic party? On this question there is a divergence of opinion among the authors. D'Annibale (1815–1892),[41] De Becker (1857–1936),[42] Vlaming (†1935),[43] Gasparri

[38] Cappello, *De Sacramentis,* III, n. 76.

[39] *Canonical Procedure in Matrimonial Cases,* p. 400.

[40] Wernz-Vidal, *Ius Matrimoniale,* n. 67.

[41] *Summula Theologiae Moralis* (5. ed., 3 vols., Romae: 1908), III, n. 425.

[42] *De Matrimonio Praelectiones Canonicae* (2. ed., Lovain: Fr. Ceuterick, 1931), nn. 25, 26.

[43] *Praelectiones Iuris Matrimonii* (3. ed., 2 vols., Bussum in Hollandia, Vol. I, 1919, Vol. II, 1921), I, n. 195.

(1852–1934) [44] and Onclin [45] can be cited as favoring the opinion that such a marriage cannot take place because of the valid civil impediment affecting the unbaptized party and rendering him incapable of the marriage.

The contrary opinion has an equal array of authorities in its favor, maintaining that such a marriage can take place because the civil impediment ceases to affect the unbaptized party when marrying a baptized person. Wernz (1842–1914),[46] Wernz-Vidal (1867–1938),[47] Chelodi (1880–1922),[48] De Smet (1868–1927),[49] Cappello,[50] Payen,[51] and Dillon,[52] among others, may be cited.

The arguments of those maintaining that such a marriage can take place advance the reason that in such a case the baptized party communicates his freedom (*habilitas*) to marry, that is, the civil impediment ceases because there is a conflict between the civil law and the law of the Church, and in the conflict the law of the Church, as of the superior society, must prevail.[53] Likewise, it is argued that the same matrimonial contract cannot be ruled by two distinct powers, hence the authority of the Church must alone be considered.[54]

However, Gasparri bases his argument on canon 1036, § 3, which states that even though the impediment exists on one side, it renders marriage illicit or invalid. Admitting the authority of the civil power to establish diriment impediments for its un-

---

[44] *De Matrimonio,* I, n. 256. It is worthy of note that this author in the post-Code edition has changed his opinion, for in the edition of 1904 (I, n. 306) he maintained that such a marriage could take place.

[45] "De Regimine Matrimonii Fidelem inter et Infidelem"—*Ephemerides Theologicae Lovanienses* (Lovanii: Universitas Catholica Lovaniensis, 1924–) X (1933), 47–62.

[46] *Ius Matrimoniale,* n. 60.

[47] *Ius Matrimoniale,* n. 52.

[48] *Ius Matrimoniale,* n. 12.

[49] *De Sponsalibus et Matrimonio,* n. 438.

[50] *De Sacramentis,* III, n. 67.

[51] *De Matrimonio,* I, nn. 200–203.

[52] *Common Law Marriage,* pp. 76–83.

[53] Cappello, *loc. cit.*

[54] Cf. Payen, *op. cit.,* I, n. 202.

baptized subjects, it follows that such an impediment prevents the unbaptized subject from contracting a valid marriage.[55] Onclin,[56] moreover, denies that there is any conflict of authority in this case between the Church and the civil authority, and he contends also, that it is not repugnant that the capacity of each party may be determined by a separate law without any intrinsic contradiction. It is not required, he affirms, that the two contracting parties be subject to the same law in so far as their freedom from impediments is concerned.

These arguments, it appears, have some validity. The Church, in canons 12 and 87, admits that it has no legislative competency over the unbaptized, for they are not her members; at least in practice the Church likewise admits that the state has the right to establish impediments for the unbaptized. So when, for example, the state legislates that no girl can marry before the completion of her eighteenth year and establishes a diriment impediment to that effect, it seems that such an impediment binds her even when she wishes to marry a baptized Catholic who is canonically free. The impediment is in effect an incapacitating law, and the unbaptized person is a valid subject of that law. The unity or individuality of the marriage contract is not touched, for the civil impediment, validly established for the unbaptized party, prevents her from entering a contract unless a dispensation has been obtained from the competent civil authority.

In support of the opinion that it is within the exclusive competency of the Church to regulate such marriages, Payen [57] employs that text of the encyclical letter *Arcanum divinae*,[58] of Pope Leo XIII, in which the pope states that marriage is of itself, by its very nature, sacred and thereby it must pertain to the Church alone when one of the parties is of the faithful. But

---

[55] Gasparri, *loc. cit.*

[56] *Op. cit.*, pp. 56–57.

[57] *Op. cit.*, I, n. 202. "Nam, ex pluribus S. Sedis Decretis et nominatim ex Encyclica *Arcanum*, constat *res natura sua sacras fidelium* ad *solam* Ecclesiam pertinere, id est *solam* Ecclesiam esse competentem ubi *duplex condicio* expletur: ubi nempe agitur *primo* de re sacra, et secundo de persona, ratione baptismi, Ecclesiae subdita." Cf. Wernz-Vidal, *op. cit.*, n. 52.

[58] *Fontes*, n. 580.

to this argument and to the use of this Encyclical Onclin takes exception. For he points out that the text is referring to the marriage of Christians.[59] Certainly the context of the encyclical seems to support Onclin, since the particular point in question, the marriage between an unbaptized and a baptized person, is not considered.[60]

Wernz-Vidal propose the further argument that the exclusive competence of the ecclesiastical courts in judging marriages which involve the faithful and the unbaptized as the two parties removes all doubt as to the sole competency of the Church in regulating the marriage between the baptized and the unbaptized.[61] But again Onclin seems to have a valid refutation of the conclusion.[62] It must be admitted that the Church has an exclusive juridical competence in cases concerning the validity of a marriage between a member of the Church and an infidel. The competence of the superior society prevails over that of the inferior society in the conflict. There is "*materia de se communis*" after the marriage has taken place. But it is wrong to deduce that thereby the Church has *exclusive legislative power;* for one principle regulates legislative competence and another principle regulates judicial competence. The adage "*ius fori sequitur ius condendi legis*" cannot be applied in this sense. Certainly it is legislative power that is involved in determining at what age a subject can validly contract marriage.

While there is a response from the Holy Office that seems to indicate that it is the practice of the Holy See not to consider a civil law impediment of any effect on the infidel when the latter is marrying a baptized person with a dispensation from disparity

---

59 Onclin, *ant. cit.*, p. 59. "Textus unice agit de matrimonio Christianorum, secus enim dicendum forum etiam duorum infidelium ad ecclesiam spectare."

60 "Igitur cum matrimonium sit sua vi, sua natura, sua sponte sacrum, consentaneum est ut regatur ac temperaetur non Principum imperio sed divina auctoritate Ecclesiae, quae rerum sacrarum sola habet magisterium. Deinde consideranda sacramenti dignitas est, cuius accessione matrimonia Christianorum evasere longe nobilissima. . . . "—*Fontes,* n. 580.

61 *Op. cit.*, n. 52.

62 *Art. cit.*, p. 58.

of cult,[63] nevertheless it is clear that this response is a solution for a particular case. Since the marriage of two infidels *seemed* to be invalid because of a civil law impediment of affinity, the missionary inquired if, after the baptism of one party, it was sufficient if they renewed their consent. The response directed that a dispensation from disparity of cult and affinity should be given and that consent had to be renewed, but no mention was made of the civil law impediment, even though the other party still remained an infidel. However, the response did mention that if harm would come, then the parties should be left in good faith. In view of this latter suggestion, that the parties should be left in good faith, it was hardly the intention of the Holy Office to establish a canonical principle, but rather to solve a particular case.[64]

While favoring the opinion of those authors who declare that a diriment impediment of nonage determined by the competent civil authority renders an unbaptized person incapable of marriage until he or she had attained the specified legal age, even though marrying a canonically free baptized person, nevertheless one must admit in practice, after such a marriage has taken place, that no diocesan court could declare such a marriage invalid, because of the canonical principle that marriage enjoys the favor of law. Therefore, in case of doubt, its validity ought to be maintained until the contrary be proved,[65] and also because of the opinion of those who claim that such a marriage is valid, there would not be sufficient certitude to allow the diocesan court to declare that no marriage existed in the situation described. But in the eventuality of such a case, since it is a dubious matter, it should be sent to the Holy See for solution.[66]

---

[63] S.C.S. Off. (ad Vic. Ap. Yun-nan), 20 sept. 1854—*Collectanea SCPF*, n. 1104.

[64] Cf. Onclin (*art. cit.*, p. 60): "Attenta praxi Curiae Romanae, potius concludendum esset eandem non favere valori legis civilis in casu."

[65] Canon 1014.

[66] As Doheny remarks: (*Canonical Procedure in Matrimonial Cases*, p. 400) "In view of the discrepancy of opinion among renowned canonists in this matter, a case of this nature should be submitted to the Holy See for solution."

B. Oriental Catholics Not Bound by Ecclesiastical Impediment of the Code

Canon 1 of the Code states the general principle: " Even though in the Code of Canon Law there frequently is reference to the discipline of the Oriental Church also, it nevertheless concerns the Latin Church only and does not obligate the Oriental, unless it is treating of those matters which from the very nature of the case affect also the Oriental." [67] In as much as the impediment of nonage as determined by canon 1067 is established by merely ecclesiastical law, it follows from the above canon that it has no binding force on Oriental Catholics, but that they remain subject to their own law in this matter.[68] This point was further elucidated in a private response of the Sacred Congregation for the Oriental Church, not officially published in the *Acta Apostolicae Sedis,* but to be found in *The Ecclesiastical Review.*[69] It was asked: (1) whether Maronites who have a domicile or quasi-domicile in the United States of North America are bound by the laws of the Code of Canon Law. The reply was: In the negative according to canon 1 of the Code, without prejudice, however, to the special decrees of the Holy See relating to them, and without prejudice to the disposition of the Apostolic Letter, *Orientalium dignitas,* n. IX: " Every Oriental, while staying outside his patriarchal territory, shall be under the administration of the Latin clergy, but shall remain ascribed to his own rite." [70]

(2) Whether two Maronites who have a domicile or quasi-domicile in the United States can contract a valid marriage, even though they are bound by some impediment which has been abrogated by the Code of Canon Law but which still exists as a

---

[67] Translation from Cicognani, *Canon Law* (2. revised ed., authorized English version by Joseph O'Hara and Francis Brennan, Philadelphia: The Dolphin Press, 1935), p. 444.

[68] Cf. Cappello, *De Sacramentis,* III, n. 68; Payen, *De Matrimonio,* I, n. 196.

[69] *The American Ecclesiastical Review* (Philadelphia, 1889–1943; Baltimore, 1944–), LXXX (1929), 384–385; cf. Bouscaren, *The Canon Law Digest,* I, 4.

[70] Leo XIII, litt. ap., " *Orientalium dignitas,*" 30 nov. 1894, n. IX—*Fontes,* n. 627.

diriment impediment for Maronites. The reply was: In the negative.

(3). Whether two Maronites who have a domicile or quasi-domicile in the United States can validly contract marriage before the age of sixteen for the man and fourteen for the girl, when it is certain that they have reached the age of puberty (*malitiam supplere aetatem*). The reply was: In the affirmative.

All the Oriental Catholics, with the exception of the Maronites, consider lack of age as a diriment impediment. The age required is that of puberty, that is, fourteen years complete for men and twelve years complete for women. Similar to the pre-Code impediment for the Latin Church, the impediment is not absolute, but the condition: *"nisi malitia suppleat aetatem"* prevails.[71]

For the Maronites the law was determined in the Synod of Mount Lebanon, celebrated in the year 1736. While the required age for marriage was given as fourteen for men and twelve for women,[72] nevertheless lack of that age was considered not even an impeding impediment, though it would temporarily impede the use of marriage between spouses.[73]

Hence, even though Oriental Catholics when marrying Catholics of the Latin rite are bound by the form of marriage prescribed by the Code,[74] still their capacity and fitness for marriage on the

[71] Cappello, *De Sacramentis,* III, n. 902; Cicognani, *Canon Law,* p. 452; Cappello, "Jus Ecclesiae Latinae cum Jure Ecclesiae Orientalis Comparatum"—*Jus Pontificium* (Romae, 1921-), VII (1927), 69.

[72] "Parochus, admonitus de aliquo matrimonio in sua parochia contrahendo, primum cognoscat ex his ad quos spectat, qui et quales sint, qui matrimonium contrahere volunt: an inter eos sit aliquod canonicum impedimentum; . . . utrum sint in aetate legitima, ut vir saltem quatuordecim, mulier vero duodecim annos expleverit . . ." Constitutiones et Canones S. Synodi Montis Libani anno 1736, pars II, cap. XI, n. 6—*Coll. Lac.,* II, 161.

[73] "Praeter haec quinque impedimenta prohibentia nonnulla alia referuntur, quae praesertim matrimonii usum inter conjugatos impediunt: . . . Aetas etiam, quae, ut supra dictum est, in viro 14 et in mulier 12 annorum completorum esse debet; nam ante hoc tempus contrahere non licet, etsi episcopus in aetatis defectu ex urgenti necessitate dispensare possit, attento sponsorum temperamento et capacitate."—Constitutiones et Canones S. Synodi Montis Libani anno 1736, pars II, cap. XI, n. 9, VI—*Coll. Lac.,* II, 169.

[74] Canon 1099, § 1, Ad statutam superius formam servandam tenetur: 3.º Orientales, si cum latinis contrahant hac forma adstrictis.

ground of age must be determined not by the law of the Code, but by their own law.

C. Oriental Schismatics

Are Oriental Schismatics and heretics, that is, those who belong to the Oriental dissident churches, bound by the prescription of canon 1067? The answer to this question seems to be the subject of some controversy; for it will depend on the answer given to the more general question as to whether Oriental dissidents are bound by the matrimonial laws of the Latin Church. One authority, Dalpiaz, firmly maintains that they are,[75] while another, Herman, contends that they are not.[76] To this latter opinion is added the weighty authority of Cappello[77] and of Vermeersch-Creusen.[78]

Dalpiaz argues from canon 1 and the interpretation given it by the analytical-alphabetical index to the Code itself, which, as he admits, is not however officially or authoritatively a part of the Code. Under the word "*Orientalis*" is found the qualification: "Catholicos ritus orientalis generatim Codex non respicit." Because canon 1 refers to and explicitly exempts only Oriental Catholics, it follows that Oriental dissidents are bound by the prescriptions of the Code.[79] Quoting Gasparri at length,[80] baptized, are in and of themselves bound by the laws of the Church, and that it was not the mind of the Church that they should be exempted from the matrimonial impediments save the explicitly excepted impediment of disparity of cult or from other matrimonial laws save that which required the specified juridical form. Hence Oriental schismatics are bound by the matrimonial im-

---

75 "An Orientales Schismatici legibus matrimonialibus Ecclesiae latinae teneantur"—*Apollinaris* (Romae, 1928–), X (1937), 457–459.

76 "Regunturne Orientales dissidentes legibus matrimonialibus Ecclesiae latinae"—*Periodica de Re Morali, Canonica, Liturgica* (formerly *Periodica de Re Canonica et Morali utili Praesertim Religiosis et Missionariis* (Brugis, 1905–), XXVII (1938), 7–20.

77 *De Sacramentis,* III, n. 68.

78 *Epitome,* II, p. 194, nota 2.

79 *Art. cit.,* p. 457.

80 *De Matrimonio,* I, n. 257.

pediments of the Code.[81] It is further pointed out that the Code makes no distinction between Oriental and Occidental schismatics, as for example in canons 751, 795, 1240, 2314, etc. Historically, ever since the unhappy schism in the XI century, Oriental schismatics have been called by the name " schismatics," and the Church could not use that word in her laws without any distinction if it meant it to refer only to other schismatics and not to Oriental schismatics.[82]

The arguments which Herman proposes, however, seem to be more cogent. He readily admits Gasparri's arguments that it is the mind of the Church that dissidents be bound by her law, but denies that it is her mind that Oriental dissidents are bound by the laws of the Latin Church. Acknowledging the fact that there are no known documents issued by the Holy See which expressly or directly decide the question, he maintains that various arguments give moral certainty to his solution.[83]

Thus Pope Benedict XIV (1740–1758) stated that the Roman Pontiffs never demanded that Oriental dissidents, returning to the Catholic Faith, had to give up their own Rite and embrace the Latin Rite, but rather that they have taken special care that they should keep the rite and discipline to which they belonged before their schism.[84] In a similar manner Pope Leo XIII (1878–1903) in a plea for unity stressed the note that the Orientals were to retain their laws and privileges.[85] If Oriental schismatics were

---

[81] *Art. cit.*, p. 458.

[82] *Ibid.*, p. 459.

[83] Herman, *Art. cit.*, p. 10.

[84] Benedictus XIV, ep. encycl., *"Allatae sunt,"* 26 iul. 1755, 1845–1847 § 18—[*Bullarium Benedicti XIV Pont. Opt. Max.* (3 vols. in 4, Prati 1845–1847), IV, 255]: "Utque uno verbo compleamur omnia, in reditu Graecorum, Schismaticorumque Orientalium ad Catholicam Religionem curando, id unum Romanis Pontificibus maxime curae fuit, ut ex illorum animis radicitus evellerent Arii, Macedonii, Nestorii, Eutychis, Dioscori, Monothelitarum aliorumque errores, in quo infeliciter proruerunt; salvis tamen et intactis ritibus ac disciplina, quam ante Schisma servabant, et profitebantur, quaeque venerandis ipsorum antiquis Liturgiis, ac Ritualibus innititur; quin unquam iidem Romani Pontifices poposcerint, ut ad Catholicam Fidem redeuntes, suum Ritum dimittere et Latinum amplecti deberent . . ."

[85] Leo XIII, ep. ap. "*Praeclara,*" 20 iun. 1894, n. 7—*Fontes,* n. 625; Acta

subject to the ecclesiastical laws of the Latin Church, Herman argues, these provisions would hardly be true. Certainly they were bound to their own laws and customs before their schism. The act of schism did not bring about that change in rite or discipline which would be necessary if they were to be brought under the disciplinary laws of the Code.[86]

A particular response from the Sacred Congregation of the Propagation of the Faith, specifically mentioning Oriental schismatics as well as Catholics, declared that they were subject to apostolic constitutions in only three cases, in matters of faith and morals, in matters in which the Pope explicitly mentioned them in his constitution, and in matters in which he implicitly referred to them.[87] While this response was never authentically approved, nevertheless it has always served as the practical norm for the Roman Congregations.[88] Thus it is the practice of the Sacred Congregation of the Oriental Church in judging the validity of the marriages of dissident Oriental priests and lay persons returning to the true Faith to apply the norms of Oriental law, and not those of the Latin Church, that is, not those of the Code.[89]

However, in virtue of canon 1060, which forbids mixed marriages, Latin Catholics are strictly prohibited from contracting marriage with a member of a schismatic or heretical sect. In the event of a dispensation from this impeding impediment, it would usually be of no practical consequence if the law of the Code on age were applied, since most of the Oriental schismatics consider the lesser age of puberty as sufficient to contract a valid

---

Sanctae Sedis (41 vols., Romae 1865–1908), XIII (1894), 201 (hereafter cited as *ASS*) : "Vera coniunctio inter christianos est, quam auctor Ecclesiae Iesus Christus instituit voluitque, in fidei et regiminis unitate consistens. Neque est cur dubitetis, quidquam propterea vel Nos vel successores Nostros de iure vestro, de patri-archalibus privilegiis, de rituali cuiusque Ecclesiae consuetudine detracturos . . ."

[86] Herman, *ibid.*, p. 12.

[87] S.C. de Prop. Fide, 4 iun. 1631—*Fontes,* n. 4449.

[88] Herman, *ibid.*, p. 14; Cappello, *De Sacramentis,* III, n. 68.

[89] Cf. Cappello, *loc. cit.*

marriage. But in passing judgment on the validity of a previously contracted marriage involving an Oriental dissident and the impediment of nonage, care must be taken to investigate the exact demands of the particular law, for on this, and not on the law of the Code, will the validity or invalidity hinge.

CHAPTER IV

Cessation of the Impediment of Nonage

Article 1: *The Computation of Age*

The manner of determining the necessary minimum age at which a man or woman can validly enter marriage, that is, precisely when the impediment of nonage ceases to bind, merits some consideration. It must be admitted that there is usually a margin of safety to preclude the necessity for exact calculation. This is especially true in this country where marriage will hardly ever be contracted at the minimum age allowed by the general law of the Church. None the less it can happen that the validity or the invalidity of a particular marriage may depend on whether exactness in the computation of the age as demanded by Canon Law was followed.[1]

In the present law it is explicitly stated that the man cannot enter marriage before he has completed his sixteenth year, and that the woman cannot do so before she has completed her fourteenth year.[2] The impediment of nonage, then, ceases upon the completion of the respective years.[3] This point is self-evident, as Cappello succinctly comments: "*ut palam est.*"[4]

In a similar manner the old law demanded that the age of fourteen and of twelve had to be complete (*nisi malitia supplet aetatem.*)[5]

[1] Cf. "The Impediment of Nonage,"—*The Ecclesiastical Review CV* (1941), 42.

[2] Canon 1067, § 1.

[3] But if the marriage has been invalidly contracted before the canonical age, the cessation of the impediment does not automatically convalidate the marriage. Cf. *infra,* p. 74.

[4] *De Sacramentis,* III, n. 338.

[5] C. 3, X, *de desponsatione impuberum,* IV, 2, ". . . eum esse puberum qui XIV annos implevit . . ."; also cc. 6, 10, 11 *h. t.*

But just when that age was complete was subject to various opinions in the pre-Code period. Some of the earlier canonists, Hostiensis (†1271) for example, taught that a moral completion of the required age for marriage was sufficient. By that they meant that the Roman Law principles of "*minimum pro nihilo reputatur,*" "*quod parum distat a re, nihil distare videtur,*" were applicable.[6] If two or three days were lacking before the completion of the necessary age it was of no consequence, and the marriage could be validly contracted. This opinion, however, had but few advocates in the post-Tridentine period. Its validity was questioned and denied by Sanchez (1550–1610).[7]

A more common opinion, while still maintaining that a moral completion of the age was sufficient for the contracting of marriage, understood moral completion in a different sense. As distinct from physical completion, it meant that in computing a period of time the last day was considered complete when begun.[8] A final and stricter opinion was maintained by Reiffenstuel (1641–1703),[9] who declared that the time had to be complete physically, that is, it was to be computed "*de momento in momentum.*" The last day was not to be considered complete when merely begun. According to Feije (1820–1894),[10] it was this latter opinion that had to be followed in practice. While he did not state his reason, it is clear that the safer opinion had to be followed when the validity of a sacrament was involved.[11] But if a

---

[6] Hostiensis, *Commentaria,* lib. IV, tit. II, c. s.v. "*implevit*"*;* Guttierrez, *De Matrimonio,* cap. IV, n. 18—apud De Justis, *De Disputationibus Matrimonialibus,* lib. III, cap. VIII, n. 40.

[7] *De Matrimonio,* lib. VII, disp. 104, n. 1.

[8] Schmalzgrueber (*Ius Canonicum Universum,* lib. IV, tit. II, n. 60): ". . . non tamen aetas ista et annum esse completum omnino physice, sed sufficit is moraliter; quo differt matrimonium a sponsalibus; in matrimonio enim propter specialem illius favorem ultima dies inchoata pro completa habetur." Sanchez, *loc. cit.;* Altimarus, *Tractatus de Nullitate* (Neapoli, 1582, rub. XI, qu. IV, n. 3; Pallottini, *Collectio,* s.v. *Matrimonium quoad Impedimentum Dirimens Aetatis,* XII, p. 534, n. 11; Wernz, *Ius Matrimoniale,* n. 321.

[9] *Ius Ecclesiasticum Universum,* lib. IV, tit. II, n. 12.

[10] *De Impedimentis et Dispensationibus Matrimonialibus,* n. 532.

[11] Tanquerey, *Synopsis Theologiae Moralis et Pastoralis,* II, 432.

marriage had already taken place, and in the computation of the minimum age of either of the parties a moral computation had been used, it could not be declared null on that ground without a prior consultation of the Holy See, for a marriage already contracted enjoyed the favor of law.[12]

The Code, however, has removed this problem from the realm of opinion. By establishing general norms it has definitely settled the question and has determined the exact manner in which the age shall be computed. These norms must be followed in all matters involving a consideration of the element of time except with reference to the laws of liturgy, or whenever a special provision may be made. This is specified by canon 31, the first canon of the title on the computation of time: " Time is to be reckoned according to the rules of the following canons, unless a different method is expressly provided; the manner of computing time in liturgical laws remains unchanged." [13] Since canon 1067 does not contain any exception or make any such special provision, the general norms must be followed.

In so far as a person's age is to be computed from the day of birth,[14] the starting point for the computation of the age is implicitly specified, and hence canon 34, § 3 is to be followed.

C. 34 § 3. "If time consists of one or several months or years, one or several weeks, or several days, and the starting point is explicitly or implicitly specified, the following rules obtain:

1°. The month or years are to be taken according to the calendar;

2°. If the starting point coincides with the beginning of the day, e.g. two months' vacation from the fifteenth of August, the first day is to be counted in the number of days and the time expires with the beginning of the day of the same number;

---

[12] Feije, *loc. cit.*, Gasparri, *De Matrimonio* (3. ed. 1904) I, 549.

[13] Translation from Cicognani, *Canon Law,* p. 672.

[14] S.C.S. Off. (ad Vic Ap. Chan-si), 7 maii 1890—*Fontes,* n. 1122; *Collectanea SCPF,* n. 1730.

3°. If the starting point does not coincide with the beginning of the day, e.g., the fourteenth year of age, the year of novitiate, eight days after the vacancy of a bishopric, the days for appeal, etc., the first day is not to be counted and the time expires with the end of the last day of the same number.[15]

Since birth cannot exactly coincide with the beginning of the day in the sense of section 2 of the above quoted canon, the day of birth is not included in the calculation and the norm of section 3 must be followed. The boy will then have completed his sixteenth year and have attained the minimum age for marriage on the expiration of his sixteenth birthday anniversary. By way of illustration, a boy born on December 9, 1943, completes his sixteenth year at the end of December 9, 1959. Precisely at the moment after midnight the impediment of nonage ceases to bind, and he is, at least on the grounds of age, canonically fitted for marriage on December 10, 1959.

It must be noted that time must be measured physically and does not admit or allow any slightness of matter.[16] To emphasize this point Wernz-Vidal remark that if one day is lacking, or even a few hours, before the completion of the required age, a marriage contracted is entirely invalid because of the juridical incapacity of the party, unless, of course, a dispensation was obtained.[17]

This age, moreover, must be measured in solar years, not lunar years. This point was certified in a response of the Holy Office to the Vicar Apostolic of Chan-si, China. Disturbed because some marriages had been contracted with the minimum age being calculated by lunar years, the Vicar Apostolic had sought a sanation for these marriages. The Holy Office responded on May 7,

[15] Translation from Cicognani, *op. cit.*, p. 685.

[16] Maroto (*Institutiones Iuris Canonici ad normam Novi Codicis* [2 vols., Vol. I, 3. ed. Romae: apud Commentarium pro Religiosis, 1921], I, 257): "Tempus computatur physice, non moraliter; quare heic non datur parvitas materiae."

[17] *Ius Matrimoniale*, n. 207.

1890, that the sanation was not required, but that thenceforth the age was to be measured only by solar years. If that was not possible, then the age was to be computed according to the lunar year, with a month added for each year.[18] Dubé maintains that this prescription holds even after the Code in virtue of Canon 6, 2°, since the Code has made no change with reference to the use of the calendar.[19] Payen also maintains the same opinion.[20] However, Dubé testifies that it is the Gregorian calendar that is now used practically everywhere throughout the civilized world.[21] This calendar is based on solar years, that is, the year is based entirely on the motion of the earth around the sun.[22] It is only among the Moslems and in some parts of China that a lunar calendar is still in use, and even in China the legal calendar is the Gregorian.[23] Payen, who is familiar with conditions in China, notes that tables have been prepared which show the corresponding age in solar years for lunar years.[24] So the problem is more theoretical than real at the present time.

ARTICLE 2: *Dispensation from the Impediment of Nonage*

Although the ordinary means by which the impediment of nonage ceases and the person becomes canonically free to marry is the attainment of the required age, there remains an extraordinary means by which a subject of the law may be released from its obligation. It is by dispensation. The natural law, as has been previously explained, makes no specific demand in regard to the age of the parties of the matrimonial contract other than that they have attained a maturity of mind and judgment sufficient

---

18 S.C.S. Off. (ad Vic. Ap. Chan-si), 7 maii 1890—*Fontes* 1122; *Collectanea SCPF*, n. 1730.

19 Dubé, *The General Principles for the Reckoning of Time in Canon Law,* The Catholic University of America Canon Law Studies, n. 144 (Washington, D. C.: The Catholic University of America Press, 1941), p. 197.

20 *De Matrimonio,* I, n. 941.

21 *Op. cit.*, p. 11.

22 Dubé, *op. cit.*, p. 8.

23 Dubé, *op. cit.*, p. 195.

24 *De Matrimonio,* I, n. 941.

to give the essential matrimonial consent. From this requirement there can be no question of a dispensation, since it derives from the natural law itself. But over and above that minimum, the impediment is of ecclesiastical law, and hence the possibility of a dispensation, or as canon 80 defines it, "a relaxation of the law in a particular case," is present.

Under the old law, marriage could take place even before the boy had completed his fourteenth year and the girl her twelfth year, if the parties had actually attained to puberty and had a sufficient mental maturity. In such an instance they did not need a dispensation, even though they were below the legally presumed age of puberty or the requisite age for marriage, but it was enough that they obtained permission from their ordinary who verified the attainment of the twofold condition, that is, "*potentia ad generandum et prudentia,*" which included knowledge of the nature of marriage, its sacredness, perpetuity and indissolubility.[25] That this was a permission and not a dispensation was clearly set forth by Pope Benedict XIV: [26]

> "The faculty of contracting marriage before the prescribed time, as often as '*malitia supplet aetatem*' comes from the very disposition of the laws and the canons. The bishop himself and the local ordinary by his own right can pronounce upon that question which is one of fact . . . consequently he can give permission for the marriage; it is not necessary to have recourse to the Holy See, except for a greater solemnity of the acts and in order that no occasion of doubt may arise about the validity of the marriage in view of the lower age at which it was contracted . . . The canonists teach that the right is cumulative between the Holy See and the ordinary to judge and pronounce on this point . . ."

Fagnanus (1598–1678) went so far as to say that it would be wrong for a bishop to refuse permission for a boy or a girl to marry, if in them there were fulfilled the conditions required as to maturity, since by law they had a right to marry. After man's

---

[25] Sanchez, *De Matrimonio,* lib. VII, disp. 104, n. 21.

[26] Benedictus XIV, const. "*Magnae Nobis,*" 29 iun. 1748, § 9—*Fontes,* n. 387; *Collectanea SCPF,* n. 364. Writer's translation.

fall, marriage was secondarily a remedy for concupiscence, and it was a Pauline precept that one who could not remain continent should marry. By denying permission for one who was fit for marriage, the bishop would be denying the remedy for concupiscence established by the natural and divine law.[27]

The conditional nature of the pre-Code impediment made the necessity of a dispensation practically non-existent, but still the authors considered the possibility. The general principle was clear. Since the impediment was of human and ecclesiastical law, the Pope as superior of that law could relax it in a particular case for a just cause.[28]

There were even some weighty authors who maintained that bishops could dispense from the impediment of nonage under certain circumstances, when the cause was most urgent, such as the promotion of peace, in a case in which the persons bound by the impediment were close to the legitimate age, but in which there was a real doubt as to whether or not the conditions of "*malitia supplet aetatem*" were fulfilled. In such circumstances bishops could grant a dispensation.[29] While fundamentally they agreed that bishops had no direct power over the common law, to which they were inferior and subject, and from which consequently they could not dispense by their own power, yet they maintained that the Decretal law itself granted to the bishops the right to dispense from the impediment of nonage under such circumstances, for it forbade marriage before the legitimate age, but with the expressed exception, "nisi forte aliqua urgentissima necessitate interveniente, utpote pro bono pacis." [30] As Barbosa

---

[27] Fagnanus, *Commentaria,* lib. IV, tit. 11, c. 9, n. 39.

[28] Cf. Sanchez, *De Matrimonio,* lib. II, disp. 40, n. 1; lib. VIII, disp. 16, n. 16; Schmalzgrueber, *Ius Ecclesiasticum Universum,* lib. IV, tit. XVI, nn. 59, 66; Wernz, *Ius Matrimoniale,* n. 323.

[29] Sanchez, *op. cit.,* lib. VII, disp. 104, n. 12; Schmalzgrueber, *op. cit.,* lib. IV, tit. II, n. 54; Leurenius, *Forum Ecclesiasticum in quo Ius Canonicum Universum Explicatur* (5 vols. in 3, Venetiis, 1729), lib. IV, tit. II, n. 137; De Justis, *De Dispensationibus Matrimonialibus,* lib. II, cap. II; Barbosa, *Pastoralis Sollicitudinis, sive De Officio et Potestate Episcopi Descriptio* (Lugduni, 1656), p. 402.

[30] C. 2, X, *de desponsatione impuberum,* IV, 2.

(1589–1649) remarked,[31] " . . . in that text the Supreme Pontiff (Pope Nicholas I) did not reserve the dispensation to himself, he seemed to grant it to the bishops, according to the principle that the power of dispensation is understood as granted to the bishops, if the Pope had not expressly reserved it to himself." However, Pope Benedict XIV relying on the more common canonical doctrine asserted that the right to grant a dispensation to one who was not yet fitted for the "*copula carnalis*" belonged exclusively (*privative*) to the Holy See.[32]

De Justis asserted (†ca. 1700) that the impediment of nonage was in the category of those from which the Holy See was not wont to dispense.[33] However, he did cite the examples of Pope Gregory XV (1621–1623) and Pope Clement VIII (1592–1605) granting a dispensation. The rescript of the dispensation granted by Pope Gregory XV may be found in Pyrrhus (†1686).[34] It is noteworthy that it was only a dispensation "*ad cautelam*," for the rescript indicated that the necessary conditions ("*malitia supplet aetatem*") were fulfilled. The boy involved was a nephew of the pope, aged eleven and a prince. The girl was of a similar age. But the isolated example of a dispensation granted under the pre-Code law only indicates the possibility of a dispensation, and does not alter the judgment that the Church was not wont to dispense, or that the Church dispensed only very rarely (*rarissime*).[35]

A private cause, that is, one based on the benefit of the individual contemplating the marriage contract, was never a sufficient reason for the extraordinary relaxation of the law; but a public cause, such as the peace of two nations, or of a kingdom, of a city or of families, was required.[36] Moreover, the Sacred

---

[31] *Loc. cit.* Writer's translation.

[32] Benedictus XIV, const., "*Magnae nobis*," 29 iun. 1748, § 9—*Fontes*, n. 387; cf. Wernz, *Ius Matrimoniale*, n. 323.

[33] *De Dispensationibus Matrimonialibus*, lib. III, cap. VIII, nn. 53, 54.

[34] *Praxis Dispensationum Apostolicarum ex Solidissimo Romanae Curiae Stylo* (Venetiis, 1735), lib. IV, cap. III, n. 18.

[35] Schmalzgrueber, *op. cit.*, lib. IV, tit. II, n. 50; Feije, *De Impedimentis et Dispensationibus Matrimonialibus*, n. 684.

[36] Cf. Gasparri, *De Matrimonio* (3. ed., 1904) I, n. 561.

Congregation of the Holy Office had occasion to respond that it was not expedient to give faculties to a certain Vicar Apostolic to dispense from the impediment of age.[37]

Further evidence that the pre-Code impediment of nonage was one from which the Church was not accustomed to grant a dispensation can be found in the special norms given to the Sacred Congregation of the Sacraments subsequent to the reorganization of the Roman Curia by the Constitution "*Sapienti Consilio*" of Pope Pius X in 1908. The only major impediments for which a dispensation was wont to be granted, if there was a legitimate cause, were certain degrees of consanguinity and affinity, and crime resulting from adultery in conjunction with a promise of future marriage.[38] The impediment of nonage was not listed among these impediments. So it does not seem to be an unwarranted conclusion that from this impediment it was the mind of the Church not to dispense.

Because of the change made by the Code, however, on the age required for marriage, advancing the age by two years and removing the condition, "*nisi malitia supplet aetatem,*" which the pre-Code law contained, it seems that a necessary departure must be made from norms used regarding the possibility of a dispensation from the impediment and from the judgments of the pre-Code authors on this point. While it still remains true that the occasion for the need of a dispensation will not be frequent, nevertheless the new law makes the occasion for a dispensation more probable.

Cappello,[39] while granting the possibility of a papal dispensation from the impediment if the person has a sufficient maturity of

---

[37] S.C.S. Off., resp. (Tchely-Meridio-occid.) 21 nov. 1866: "Quoad facultatem dispensandi super impedimento aetatis in matrimoniis contrahendis ab impuberibus intelligentibus vim et naturam matrimonii, et nondum actu maturis ad copulam consummandum, *non expedire;* eidem tamen communicetur ea pars Constitutionis Bened. XIV *Magnae Nobis* ad rem faciens, et instructio mense maio huius anni data ad Vic. Ap. Hunanensem."—*Collectanea SCPF* (Romae, 1893), n. 1382.

[38] Ordo Servandus in S. Congregationibus, Tribunalibus, officiis Romanae Curiae, 29 sept. 1908, Pars II, *Normae Peculiares,* cap. VII, art. III, nn. 19, 20—*Fontes,* n. 6460; cf. *AAS,* I (1909), 91.

[39] *De Sacramentis,* III, n. 338.

mind and judgment to give proper matrimonial consent, remarks that the dispensation is very rarely (*rarissime*) granted, and then only for a public cause. Except in danger of death, a private cause is not sufficient. But from his references it is clear that he is basing his conclusions on the pre-Code law, and has not taken into consideration the change made in the law. In a similar manner De Smet (1868–1927) [40] admitting that the Church rarely and reluctantly (*raro et aegre*) dispenses from the impediment, concludes that it should be numbered among those from which the Church is not wont to dispense.

However, Gasparri [41] and Wernz-Vidal,[42] among others, rightfully indicate that the Church is milder and more lenient in its attitude towards a dispensation under the present law than previously. Payen [43] insists that the Church is wont to dispense, provided that the parties have completed the age formerly determined in the old law. He adds that those authors exaggerate who without making any distinctions say that the Church only very rarely (*rarissime*) dispenses from the impediment of nonage. In substantiation of this judgment, Payen has irrefutable evidence in an indult which the Vicars Apostolic of China sought and obtained from the Sacred Congregation of the Propagation of the Faith to dispense from this impediment.[44]

Even though the particular indult is extraordinary, it is of importance in so far as it indicates that the Church is wont to dispense under limited conditions. However, it must be noted

[40] *De Sponsalibus et Matrimonio,* n. 547.

[41] *De Matrimonio,* I, n. 499.

[42] *Ius Matrimoniale,* n. 212.

[43] *De Matrimonio,* I, n. 958.

[44] "In Sinis, Vicariis Apostolicis qui indultum rogaverunt, S.C. de P. Fide, 'cum iis . . . qui *post* promulgationem Codicis sponsalia iniverint . . . , potestatem tribuit, iustis exsistentibus causis, dispensandi . . . in 25 casibus,' vel pluribus, v.g. 50, 'pro suo prudenti arbitrio et conscientia, *dummodo* tamen sponsi . . . ad antiqui iuris aetatem pervenerint.' "—Payen, *De Matrimonio,* I, nn. 978, et 959; cf. Vermeersch-Creusen, *Epitome,* II, n. 337: "Etsi facultas dispensandi super aetate ne in maxima quidem omnium formula Facultatum reperitur, nobis compertum est eam pro regionibus quibusdam missionum ad certum numerum concedi. In hac re satis periculosa, opportunum videtur ut Ordinarius suam facultatem ne deleget."

that the ordinary faculties which the Sacred Congregations usually grant to local ordinaries either through the Sacred Congregation of the Propagation of the Faith or through the Sacred Consistorial Congregation do not include the faculty of dispensing from this impediment, but specifically except it and classify it, in its exception, with the impediments arising from the sacred order of priesthood and from affinity in the direct line when the marriage which gave rise to this impediment was consummated.[45] But the ordinary faculties granted to some Apostolic Nuncios and Delegates include the faculty of dispensing in a limited number of cases from all diriment impediments of ecclesiastical law, except from the impediments arising from affinity in a direct line when the marriage was consummated, and from sacred orders and solemn religious profession.[46] Hence, in so far as the impediment of nonage arises from ecclesiastical law, it seems that the Apostolic Delegate in this country could grant a dispensation.

The possibility, then, of a dispensation from this impediment under the present law is not only theoretical, but also practical in so far as it can actually be obtained, if the occasion and sufficiently grave causes warrant it. In the case of nonage, as for any dispensation, the general principle of canon 84 must be observed: " No dispensation from an ecclesiastical law should be granted without a just and reasonable cause, which should be in

---

[45] Cf. Formulae Facultatum quas S.C. de Prop. Fide Ordinariis in terris missionum procurat . . . n. 21. "Dispensandi, canonicis exsistentibus causis, super impedimentis matrimonialibus sive minoris sive maioris gradus, tam publicis quam occultis, etiam multiplicibus, iuris tamen ecclesiastici; exceptis impedimentis provenientibus ex sacro presbyteratus ordine, ex defectu praescriptae aetatis et ex affinitate in linea recta, consummato matrimonio . . ."—cf. Vermeersch-Creusen, *Epitome,* I, n. 873 (appendix I).

[46] Index facultatum quas, pro locis missionis suae, Nuntiis, Internuntiis et Delegatis Apostolicis, penes civitates seu nationes, post Codicis Iuris Canonici Publicationem tribuere SSmus Dominus Noster decrevit, ceteris abrogatis.

Caput III, Facultates circa matrimonium . . . n. 30: "Dispensandi pro . . . vicibus ex gravi causa ab omnibus impedimentis dirimentibus matrimonium, iuris tamen ecclesiastici, sive publicis sive occultis, sive minoris sive maioris gradus, iis tamen exceptis quae ex affinitate in linea recta consummato matrimonio, ex ordine sacro et sollemni professione religiosa proveniunt."—cf. Vermeersch-Creusen, *op. cit.,* I, n. 872 (appendix I).

due proportion to the gravity of the law from which the dispensation is given; otherwise the dispensation granted by an inferior is both illicit and invalid."[47] But over and above this general norm, it is of special significance and importance that the impediment of nonage is by virtue of canon 1042, § 3, an impediment of major degree, which concept has its application precisely in regard to the obtaining of a dispensation.[48]

In the Instruction issued by the Sacred Congregation of the Sacraments on June 29, 1941, regarding the rules to be observed by the pastor in conducting the canonical investigations before admitting the parties to the celebration of marriage,[49] it is pointed out that a canonical or a just cause, proportionate to the gravity of the impediment and actually existing, is required for the *validity* of a dispensation from impediments of major degree.[50] As the Instruction itself indicates, it is simply reiterating the requirements of two previous Instructions, one issued by the Sacred Congregation of the Propagation of the Faith on May 9, 1877,[51] the other issued by its own authority on August 1, 1931.[52]

While this latter Instruction was concerned primarily with the impediment of consanguinity, it makes a general reference to dispensations: ". . . the Church has established matrimonial impediments in order to provide more effectively for the proper establishment and regulation of family life and for the procreation and education of children. The pastors should therefore try to restrain the faithful from too easily asking for matrimonial dispensations, especially those which concern major impediments, unless truly grave and urgent reasons require it . . ."[53] The Instruction, moreover, indicated what causes would justify a

---

[47] Translation from Cicognani, *Canon Law,* p. 852.

[48] Cf. Wernz-Vidal, *Ius Matrimoniale,* n. 147; Gasparri, *De Matrimonio,* I, n. 211.

[49] *AAS,* XXXIII (1941), 297 ff.; *The Jurist* (Washington, D. C., 1941–), II (1942), No. 1 (January) Supplement; Bouscaren, *The Canon Law Digest,* II, 253.

[50] S.C. de Sacramentis, instr. 29 iun. 1941, n. 5, g.—*AAS,* XXXIII (1941), 302.

[51] *Collectanea, SCPF,* n. 1470; *Fontes,* n. 4890.

[52] *AAS,* XXIII (1932), 413; Bouscaren, *op. cit.,* I, 514.

[53] Bouscaren, *loc. cit.*

dispensation from the impediment of consanguinity. The fact that there is some parity between this impediment and that of nonage in so far as they are both established for the social, moral and physical well being of human society appears to justify the adoption of these norms when there is question of a dispensation from the impediment of nonage.

In the Instruction it is insisted that the cause be serious:

> "Let the Most Excellent Bishops, therefore, in asking for the aforesaid dispensations, regard as just and proportionately grave only such causes as are held legitimate in view of canonical provisions and the constant and long continued practice of the Holy See, such as the preventing of notable scandal, the settlement of important questions affecting the succession of property, or relief of involved or very distressing family conditions. And therefore, they should regard as insufficient the causes which are usually alleged for other impediments even of the major class, namely, the smallness of the place, the want of dowry, and others of the same kind; except in cases where these, although individually insufficient, yet when taken cumulatively constitute so grave a reason as to make the dispensation advisable . . ."[54]

What is more, it is recommended that the bishop himself in his own handwriting, when it can be done without grave inconvenience, should write a letter to the Sacred Congregation reporting the canonical causes and other circumstances in consideration of which he judges affirmatively regarding the advisability of the dispensation. At least, the petition for the dispensation should be signed by the bishop and recommended by him in a special manner.

It is evident that but few of the sixteen classical causes suggested by the Instruction of 1877 as the more common canonical reasons for a dispensation would have application at the present time to the impediment of nonage.[55]

---

[54] Bouscaren, *loc. cit.*

[55] Cf. *Collectanea SCPF,* n. 1470. For an evaluation and explanation of these causes, cf. Quigley, *A Summary of the Canon Law on Matrimonial Impediments and Dispensations* (2. ed., Philadelphia: The Dolphin Press, 1942), p. 10; Payen, *De Matrimonio,* I, nn. 738–759; Gasparri, *De Matrimonio,* I, nn. 295–323; Cappello, *De Sacramentis,* III, nn. 259–267.

By way of an example of a sufficiently grave reason for a dispensation from this impediment Gasparri[56] cites "*si copula cum praegnantia intercesserit,*" but even in this instance, while the cause would probably be sufficient to obtain the dispensation, circumstances and prudence may well dictate other reasons why the unfortunate girl, still below the age of 14, should not marry, and why a dispensation should consequently not be sought.

If a dispensation from the impediment of nonage should be granted, it follows from the fact of its being an impediment of major degree that the validity of the dispensation will depend on the truth of the reasons indicated and on the existence of the causes expressed in the petition. This point is emphasized in the 1941 Instruction of the Sacred Congregation of the Sacraments:[57] ". . . when the dispensation is obtained (and this must be carefully noted), *before the execution of the rescript,* it must be *certain* that the reason actually exists, else there is danger that the dispensation will be invalid (cc. 38 and 41)." In this the Instruction is not exceeding the demands of the Code itself. In virtue of canons 39 and 40 the truth of the reasons expressed in the petition for any rescript is an essential condition on which depends the validity of the favor granted. It is only dispensations from impediments of minor degree that are not vitiated by the withholding of truth (*subreptio*) or the exposition of falsehood (*obreptio*).[58]

In addition to this means of obtaining a dispensation from the impediment of nonage directly from the Holy See, or from the one who has a special indult to grant it, there is also the possibility of others granting it in virtue of the power given to them by the law itself under specified conditions. Thus the local ordinaries can dispense by virtue of canons 81,[59] 1043 and 1045 under the circumstances postulated in these canons. Similarly the pastor, the priest lawfully delegated to assist at marriage, and

[56] *Op. cit.,* I, n. 499.

[57] S.C. de Sacramentis, instr. 29 iun. 1941, n. 5, g—*AAS,* XXXIII (1941), 302; Bouscaren, *op. cit.,* II, 259.

[58] Canon 1054.

[59] Pont. Cod. Comm., respons, 27 iul. 1942, ad I—*The Jurist,* III (1943), 155; Bouscaren, *The Canon Law Digest,* II, 45.

the confessor can employ the right given them in canons 1044 and 1045, provided, of course, that the definitely circumscribed conditions are verified. It need hardly be emphasized that this right to dispense is conditioned on the fact that the impediment arises from ecclesiastical law, that is, when the parties have a sufficient maturity of mind and judgment to give a true matrimonial consent.

Mention may also be made of the possibility of invoking the power, conferred on ordinaries in canon 15, of dispensing when a "*dubium facti*" exists. Since this impediment is classified as one which the Holy See is accustomed to dispense, it would be possible for the ordinary to dispense if there were a real doubt as to whether the party to the marriage has actually attained the necessary age, and there were moreover no means of clearing up the doubt in view of the fact that no document or witnesses would be available.

ARTICLE 3: *Proof of the Cessation of the Impediment—Prenuptial Investigation*

Because of the sanctity of marriage, to protect it from all danger of irreverence or invalidity, the Church has in the past as well as in the present insisted that every provision be made to assure its valid and licit reception. The Code is summarizing the history of this solicitude when with legal brevity it states in canon 1019 that before a marriage is celebrated it must be ascertained that there is no obstacle to its valid and licit celebration.

It is further indicated that the pastor who has the right to assist at a marriage must investigate at a suitable time beforehand whether there is any obstacle to the marriage. This he should do by questioning each party separately and prudently inquiring whether either is hindered by any impediment.[60] It is a serious and grave obligation that rests with the pastor both in virtue of his office and by reason of the preceptive nature of the ecclesiastical law.[61] To stress the obligation and emphasize the importance

[60] Canon 1020.

[61] Cf. Donovan, *The Pastor's Obligation in Pre-Nuptial Investigation*, The Catholic University of America Canon Law Studies, n. 115 (Washing-

of this prenuptial investigation, the Holy See has subsequent to the promulgation of the Code issued two instructions on this point, the first in 1921 especially emphasizing the requirement of a baptismal certificate; [62] the second in 1941 suggesting more exact norms to be followed in the investigation.[63]

It must be conceded, however, that of all the impediments to marriage there is none that can be more easily investigated than the impediment of nonage. Under ordinary circumstances it will offer no problem for the pastor to ascertain with moral certitude that the parties are free from this impediment. As Donovan remarks: "Usually the observant pastor will be able to declare from a glance at the parties whether they have reached the legal age for marriage. However he should not rely too much on his observation of the parties, for many persons are actually younger and others are actually older than their appearance indicates." [64]

While the judgment from personal observation is not without some value, yet the pastor in fulfilling the law of prenuptial investigation must have further substantiation. Among the questions in the appendix of the Instruction of 1941 issued by the Sacred Congregation of the Sacraments to be asked of the parties under oath, the first one deals with the age of the parties.[65] So the pastor, after explaining the sanctity of an oath and the gravity of the penalties for perjury, will have a sworn statement of the age of the parties. Furthermore, if either party or both are minors and the pastor is not certain of the absence of all obstacles, the Instruction requires that the parents or guardians be questioned under oath, as to the day, month, year of birth of the party.[66]

---

ton, D. C.: The Catholic University of America, 1938), p. 83; Gasparri, *De Matrimonio,* I, n. 130; Cappello, *De Sacramentis,* III, n. 146.

[62] S.C. de Sacramentis, instr. 4 iul. 1921—*AAS,* XIII (1921), 348–349; Bouscaren, *The Canon Law Digest,* I, 497–498.

[63] S.C. de Sacramentis, instr. 29 junii 1941—*AAS,* XXXIII (1941), 297 ff.; Bouscaren, *op. cit.* II, 253 seq.; *The Jurist,* II (1942), No. 1 (January), Supplement.

[64] *Op. cit.,* p. 166.

[65] S.C. de Sacramentis, instr. 29 iun. 1941, Appendix, allegatum I, n. 1.—*AAS,* XXXIII (1941), 307.

[66] *Ibid.,* Appendix, allegatum III, n. 1.—*AAS.,* XXXIII (1941), 312.

To this testimony and evidence must be added that afforded by the baptismal certificate, which the Code demands as required of each party if the sacrament was not conferred in the parish of the pastor making the investigation.[67] While the primary purpose of this certificate is to insure that the sacrament was conferred and to give some evidence of the free status of the party,[68] nevertheless it will substantiate the sworn statement of the party as to his or her age. But it must be mentioned here that the baptismal certificate will not *prove* the date of birth, since that information is only accessorily contained in and not directly or primarily affirmed by the document.[69]

Even though the date of birth is usually recorded together with the date of baptism in the baptismal register, the law of the Code does not require that it be done.[70] While the evidence of the date of birth on a baptismal certificate is not of itself sufficient proof of a person's age to allow a court to declare a marriage invalid after it has been contracted, still it gives the pastor in his pre-nuptial investigation sufficient certitude to allow marriage to be contracted, especially in connection with the sworn statement of the parties themselves.

If one of the parties is unbaptized the pastor must be certain that he or she has reached the minimum age required by the civil law, for in the case of the unbaptized the presence of this factor is necessary for the validity of the marriage, as has been previously explained.[71]

But the ascertaining of the fact that the parties have attained the necessary minimum ages, although it will safeguard the validity of the marriage, does not end the pastor's obligation in relation to the impediment of nonage. The pastor has the added duty of dissuading the parties from marriage if they are below

---

[67] Cf. canon 1021, § 1.

[68] Cf. canons 470, § 2; 1103, § 2; 777, § 1; 1988.

[69] Cf. canon 1816; Wanenmacher, *Canonical Evidence in Marriage Cases,* n. 369.

[70] Canon 777, § 1: Parochi debent nomina baptizorum, mentione facta de ministro, parentibus ac patrinis, de loco ac die collati baptismi, in baptismali libro sedulo et sine ulla mora referre.

[71] Cf. *supra,* pp. 33–43.

the age at which, according to the custom of the region, marriage is usually contracted.[72] Generally, but not always or exclusively, the customary age will be that determined by the civil law.[73]

When it is two baptized persons who are involved in the marriage, it is not the civil law in its nature of an impediment that is to be considered, but the civil law inasmuch as it furnishes a norm reflecting the minimum age of a locality at which marriage is customarily contracted. Certainly the principle is clear that the state has no competency or right to establish impediments for the marriages of Christians.[74]

But the problem of the person's age as determined by the civil law becomes even more practical in regard to the obtaining of a marriage license. All the States and Territories of the United States have laws which require that a marriage license be obtained before the celebration of marriage.[75] It is to be expected that the license will be refused if the status of the parties to the marriage does not comply with the demands of the civil law. This refusal is tantamount to a denial by the state of the pastor's right to assist at such a marriage. While it is conceded that the state has a right to require that a marriage be civilly registered, since the state has a valid competency in the matter of the merely civil effects which are separable from the marriage itself,[76] the right certainly does not include also a right which authorizes the state to require a permission *before* the marriage may or can be contracted.[77]

---

[72] Cf. canon 1067, § 2.

[73] Chelodi, *Ius Matrimoniale,* n. 68; Cappello, *De Sacramentis,* III, n. 335.

[74] Cf. canons 1016, 1038.

[75] Alford, *Jus Matrimoniale Comparatum* (New York: P. J. Kenedy & Sons, 1938), n. 284; Vernier, *American Family Laws* (2 vols. Stanford University, California: Stanford University Press, 1931–1933) I, 59.

[76] Cf. Gasparri, *De Matrimonio,* I, n. 239; Cappello, *De Sacramentis,* III, n. 71, 4o.

[77] Ottaviani (*Institutiones Iuris Publici Ecclesiastici,* II, n. 337): "Insuper Status, cum habeat ius ordinandi effectus civiles, ut hi legitime tribui possint, praescribere potest ut coniuges matrimonium suum, coram Ecclesia iam valide et licite celebratum, *in publicis civitatis tabulis inscribant.* Haec inscriptio ergo supponit matrimonium iam formatum, ideoque ipsa supervenire debet, non autem antecedere matrimonialem contractum; item eadem

It is obvious that if the pastor should witness the marriage of his baptized subjects when they are canonically free even though they did neglect to obtain a civil marriage license or fell short of the civil law requirement of age, the marriage would be valid. State laws of this kind are not valid for baptized persons, for it is outside the limit of the State's competence to make such laws for the baptized. However, before proceeding in such a case the pastor would have to consult the local ordinary.[78] As Cappello remarks, it is the mind of the Church that civil laws, just in themselves but invalid because they exceed the limits of competence, should as a rule be followed, not in consequence of the laws themselves, for they do not bind, since they are invalid, but because of the precept of charity which asks that all readily preventable harm be averted for the parties and their offspring.[79] Ottaviani gives similar reasons for following the civil law prescriptions.[80] But Cappello rightly qualifies his statement with "*regulariter*," and adds that in some cases and under special circumstances at the judgment of the competent ecclesiastical

---

inscriptio concedi debet omnibus et solis matrimoniis, quae sunt coram Ecclesia valida.

Quare non licet reipublicae huic inscriptioni conditiones imponere, quarum vi alicuius existentis matrimonii recusari valeant inscriptio in civilibus tabulis . . ."

78 S.C.S. Off., resp. (ad Vic. Ap. Jamaicae), 12 ian. 1881, ad 1: "Curandum a missionariis ut matrimonium contracturi observent praescriptiones etiam civiles, quae ad ordinem moralem, quoad effectus civiles matrimonii, conservandum conducant. Quod si contingat ut missionariorum monita nihil proficiant, vel specialis occurrat difficultas; res est ad Vic. Ap. deferenda, cuius erit iudicare utrum huiusmodi sit casus ut matrimonium permitti debeat, non obstantibus civilibus praescriptionibus."—*Collectanea SCPF,* n. 1545; *Fontes,* n. 1069.

79 Cappello, *De Sacramentis,* III, n. 74; cf. Heneghan "Civil Marriage License"—*The Jurist,* III (1943), 314.

80 "Animadvertendum tamen est in praxi honestas (idest iuri naturali et divino positivo non contrarias) prohibitiones et praescriptiones civiles esse servandas; non quidem vi legum civilium, quae de se invalidae sunt, sed propter ordinatam legem caritatis avertendi a se et a prole gravia damna; qua in re Ecclesiae instructiones sequendae sunt et episcoporum dictamina quoad singulas leges civiles."—*op. cit.,* II, n. 340.

authority a marriage can, and sometimes should, be celebrated apart from the observance of the civil laws.[81]

A final consideration which may confront the pastor in his prenuptial investigation arises when the parties who contemplate marriage are still minors, that is, when they have not yet completed their twenty-first year.[82] Although this problem is not directly connected with the impediment of nonage, it has some relation to it; for the pastor has an obligation to admonish minors that they should not enter marriage without the knowledge or against the reasonable opposition of their parents. If they do not heed his advice, the pastor should not assist at their marriage without first consulting the ordinary.[83]

---

[81] *Loc. cit.*

[82] Cf. canon 88, § 1.

[83] Canon 1034.

CHAPTER V

Convalidation of a Marriage Invalidly Contracted Because of the Impediment of Nonage

The absolute necessity of persons attaining the ages for marriage prescribed by canon 1067 renders null and void any marriage attempted before the completion of the requisite ages, that is, for those persons subject to the law of the Code and not dispensed from it. The effect of the impediment is to make the parties juridically incapable of expressing a valid matrimonial consent. Neither good faith, nor ignorance of the law, nor error on the part of the persons themselves or of the priest who witnessed their marriage can supply for the extant legal incapacity.[1]

To remedy the unfortunate situation when the parties are living together in such an invalid union, there remains the possibility of a simple convalidation or a radical sanation of the marriage. The remedies of leaving the parties in good faith, when they do not know of the invalidity of their marriage,[2] or of suggesting that they live together as brother and sister,[3] while worthy of mention as possible solutions, hardly call for further treatment here, since neither of these very extraordinary solutions touches the root of the canonical problem or alters the status of the invalid marriage. When very limited circumstances allow their use, they offer a moral solution in the realm of conscience, but not for the external forum which canon law controls. A canonical remedy available as a last resort forms the basis for the next chapter, namely the obtaining of a declaration of nullity from the competent ecclesiastical court.

---

[1] Cf. canon 16, § 1.

[2] Cf. Payen, *De Matrimonio,* I, n. 966.

[3] Cappello, *De Sacramentis,* III, n. 841; Dillon, *Common Law Marriage,* p. 91.

ARTICLE 1 : *Simple Convalidation*

Under Decretal law, if one or both the parties were below the legal age for marriage, that is, of twelve years for the girl and of fourteen for the boy, and the condition of "*malitia supplet aetatem*" was not fulfilled, even though they expressed matrimonial consent "*de praesenti*" with the intention of contracting a real marriage, they were actually and by the force of the law contracting only "*sponsalia de futuro.*" The mere passing of time and the attainment of puberty or of a marriageable age did not make the contract they had entered to become the contract of marriage, unless "*copula carnalis*" or some equivalent factor indicated that the will and the intention of the parties remained unaltered.[4]

While it cannot be said that the cessation of the impediment by the lapse of time brought about an automatic convalidation of the marriage, yet the fact that the parties lived together and used marriage seemed to be sufficient to bring that about. Because there was no universal requirement in Decretal law to demand a solemn form of marriage, and inasmuch as the impediment ceased of itself, the original consent, although expressed at a time when the persons were incapable of marriage, was considered as having been renewed by the use of marriage or through some other equivalent sign. That was sufficient.

After the Council of Trent, however, in view of the enactment of the decree *Tametsi,* which forbade clandestine marriages and demanded a solemn form,[5] the problem of convalidating an invalidly contracted marriage in which one or both of the parties were below the required age took on a new aspect. By the force of this decree, wherever it was published,[6] the presence of one's own pastor, or of a properly delegated priest, along with two

---

[4] C. 1, *de sponsalibus et matrimonio,* IV, 2, in VI°.

[5] Conc. Trident., sess. XXIV, *de ref. matrim.,* c. 1.

[6] For an enumeration of places where this decree was published, cf. Wernz, *Ius Matrimoniale,* n. 162; Heneghan, "The Decree 'Tametsi' in the United States"—*The Jurist,* III (1943), 318. Subsequently, with the decree *Ne temere* issued by the Sacred Congregation of the Council on August 2, 1907 (*Fontes,* n. 4340; *ASS,* XL [1907], 527) the solemn form became necessary for all Latin Catholics.

witnesses was necessary for the contracting of a valid marriage. But even though the proper canonical form was followed, a diriment impediment, such as lack of the requisite age for marriage, still invalidated the attempted marriage. Specifically in relation to the impediment of nonage, even though the impediment had ceased of itself, nevertheless the renewal of consent before the priest and two witnesses was necessary to convalidate the invalid marriage in all cases wherein this impediment was public in character.[7] If, however, the impediment was occult, it was sufficient that the parties themselves privately and without witnesses renewed their consent.[8]

Thus the pre-Code authors recognized the possibility that this impediment could be either public or occult. The procedure necessary to convalidate such a marriage depended on the category into which the impediment fell. But the distinctions between public and occult impediments were multiple. An impediment was considered public either by its nature (*sua natura*), if it arose from a fact which was in and of itself public, or from circumstances, if as a fact it became notorious, or also if it stood practically acknowledged in the external forum. On the other hand, an impediment was occult either simply (*simpliciter*), when the fact was known only to a few discreet persons, or entirely (*omnino*), when it was known only to the parties themselves and their confessor.[7]

While these distinctions were of the utmost importance in the matter of obtaining certain dispensations, the only consideration in so far as the convalidating a marriage was concerned (which is the point at issue) was whether or not the impediment could be proved in the external forum. If such proof could be established, the impediment was considered public and the consent had to be exchanged again before the priest and two witnesses; other-

[7] Sanchez, *De Matrimonio,* lib. II, disp. 37, n. 6; *De Justis, De Dispensationibus Matrimonialibus,* lib. III, cap. VIII, n. 62; Pallottini, *Collectio,* s. v. Matrimonium quoad impedimentum dirimens aetatis, XII, 535, n. 17.

[8] Sanchez, *loc. cit.;* Schmalzgrueber, *Ius Ecclesiasticum Universum,* lib. IV, tit. XVI, n. 276; Wernz, *Ius Matrimoniale,* n. 325.

[9] Wernz, *Ius Matrimoniale,* n. 216, V; Gasparri, *De Matrimonio* (3. ed., 1904), I, nn. 259, 260.

wise the impediment was considered occult, and correspondingly a private renewal of consent was sufficient.[10]

Under the present legislation of the Code for the convalidation of marriages the same question arises, for canon 1135 states that if the impediment is public, consent must be renewed by each of the parties in the form prescribed by law. Is the impediment of nonage always public? Should it be classified as public by its very nature (*sua natura*), so that in every instance a public renewal of consent before the proper priest and witness is required to convalidate a marriage in which this impediment is involved?

Payen is of the opinion that this impediment is by its very nature public.[11] But he concedes the possibility of its being in a particular case incidentally occult if it cannot be proved in the external forum. In such a case, he says, the impediment is occult according to the definition of canon 1037.[12] Gasparri states simply that it is by its nature public.[13] But Vermeersch (1858–1936)-Creusen[14] remark that whether the impediment is public or occult will depend on whether it can be proved in the external forum, that is, on the principle of canon 1037. So these authors do not classify it as public by its very nature. Wanenmacher likewise states that, strictly taken, the impediment of nonage is not public by its nature.[15]

It is clear, however, that the problem involved is a more fundamental one that pertains not simply to the impediment of nonage, but to all impediments for the proper distinction between public and occult impediments. Under canon 1037 the Code gives one norm of distinguishing public and occult impediments: " An impediment which can be proved in the external forum is con-

---

[10] Gasparri, *loc. cit.;* S.C.C., Mohiloven, seu Teraspolen., 9 iul., 10 sept. 1881—Fontes, n. 4253; *Thesaurus Resolutionum S.C.C.*, CXL, 483.

[11] *De Matrimonio,* I, n. 964.

[12] *Op. cit.,* I, n. 965.

[13] *De Matrimonio,* I, n. 500.

[14] *Epitome,* II, n. 451, 1.

[15] *Canonical Evidence in Marriage Cases,* n. 369. His reason, however, is not based on any disagreement with the manner of distinguishing the impediment, but on the fact that age cannot be proved fully from the baptismal record.

sidered public; otherwise it is occult." But in the fourth book the Code refers to impediments public by their nature, in the event of which the promoter of justice as well as the spouses themselves have the right to impugn the validity of the marriage.[16] Vermeersch-Creusen[17] are of the same opinion, namely, that under this title of the Code (*De Matrimonio*) there is no other notion of public and occult impediments than that which involves the possibility of proof or the lack of it in the external forum. It is only under matrimonial processes that the Code holds to the old distinction between impediments public or occult by their nature.

So it does not seem proper, since it does not appear to be in accord with the mind of the Code, to classify the impediment of nonage as public by its very nature in reference to convalidation. On this point Gasparri seems to be inconsistent, for he does so classify this impediment in his treatment of nonage,[18] but at the same time he states that this distinction of impediments as public by their nature is no longer to be considered since the promulgation of the Code, at least in reference to the Third Book.[19] In the same way Payen, by calling the impediment of nonage public by its nature, is forced to say that it is also occult by the definition of canon 1037 when, by way of exception, no proof of the person's age is available.[20]

---

[16] Gasparri, *op. cit.*, I, n. 209. From his cross reference under convalidation (II, n. 1198) it seems that he would apply the same norm in this case.

[17] *Epitome*, II, n. 297, 4.

[18] *Op. cit.*, I, n. 500. "At si matrimonium ex hoc capite [impedimentum aetatis] nulliter initum fuit, non convalescit tractu temporis, sed necesse est ut novus consensus emittatur . . . et cum impedimentum *aetatis* publicum sit natura sua, consensus ab utraque parte renovandus est forma iure praescripta, ut statuit can. 1135 § 1."

[19] *Op. cit.*, I, n. 209: "Ante Codicis promulgationem DD. plura scripserunt de alia impedimentorum distinctione, nempe de impedimentis *natura sua publicis*, vel *natura sua occultis*, prout factum ex quo impedimentum oriebatur, de se publicum erat vel occultum. Codex in re tantum iudiciali lib. IV, can. 1971 § 1 n. 2 mentionem facit de impedimentis *natura sua publicis;* cum igitur de hac distinctione Codex in lib. III, agens de impedimentis, taceat omnino, putamus hanc distinctionem in dispensationibus matrimonialibus non esse amplius attendendam."

[20] *De Matrimonio*, I, n. 964.

To say that the impediment is by its nature public but in fact occult would hardly offer a solution, for that is a distinction that is not recognized after the Code by canon 1037, nor could it be used in convalidating a marriage. As Vermeersch-Creusen point out, canon 1135, § 1, is to be interpreted in the terms of canon 1037.[21]

However, it must be admitted that the question is hardly a practical one. It would be a rare exception to find a case in which age could not be proved either by documents or by witnesses. Yet it is only in the event of such an exception that the impediment could be occult. Certainly to say that it will always be public is not accurate, for the public character of the impediment will depend on the fact that proof of the impediment can be established in a particular case.[22]

But in the convalidation of marriage there are other conditions which the law of the Code explicitly postulates. The impediment must cease or be dispensed, and consent must be renewed by the party conscious of the impediment.[23] Even though the original consent was valid in the beginning according to the sole demand made by the natural law and thereafter was never revoked, nevertheless it is a requisite of ecclesiastical law that it be renewed.[24] Furthermore, the renewal of consent must be a new act of the will ratifying a marriage known to have been null from the beginning.[25]

To illustrate these principles the use of an example may prove helpful. George, a baptized Catholic, born on December 30, 1927, marries Gertrude, also a baptized Catholic, following the prescribed form before the pastor of the bride and two witnesses. Through lack of advertence to the still existing impediment of nonage the marriage takes place on December 30, 1943, George's

---

[21] *Epitome,* II, n. 451. Similarly, Payen, *De Matrimonio,* II, n. 2557.

[22] This problem will receive further consideration under the third article of this chapter in which the right of the promoter of justice in impugning the validity of a marriage involving the impediment of nonage is studied. Cf. *infra,* pp. 91 ff.

[23] Canon 1133, § 1.

[24] Canon 1133, § 2.

[25] Canon 1134.

sixteenth birthday. Even though both parties express a true matrimonial consent which is valid from the exclusive viewpoint of the natural law, nevertheless the marriage is invalid by reason of the impediment of nonage. George was juridically incapable of giving marriage consent on that day. The very next day the impediment has ceased of itself, but that fact does not automatically convalidate the marriage. Then he is no longer bound by the impediment. Through ignorance he may continue to cohabit with Gertrude and use the rights of marriage. But these facts do not rectify or regularize the situation. Until he becomes aware that his marriage is invalid and was invalid from the beginning and then renews his consent by a new act of his will, the marriage will remain invalid. If the day of his birth has been officially recorded, or if there are witnesses who can testify and prove the day of his birth, the impediment must be considered public, and George and Gertrude must renew their consent in the prescribed form, that is, before the duly authorized priest and two witnesses.

ARTICLE 2: *Radical Sanation*

While the canonical commentators, both those who wrote before the Code and those who have written after its promulgation, do not seem to treat expressly of radical sanation as a means of convalidating a marriage invalidly contracted by reason of the impediment of nonage, it still remains a possible, if extraordinary, solution.[26] Under the pre-Code law, in the absence of any positive evidence that this remedy was ever employed, it could be argued that if it was ever used it was indeed most exceptional. The nature of the impediment under the old law, the legal presumption which militated against the fact of consent as given by one who had not attained the age of puberty, and the fact that even a simple dispensation was only very rarely granted, justifiably form the basis for such an argument.[27] But under the present law,

[26] Gasparri, to illustrate the principles involved in radical sanation, cites as an example a marriage invalidly contracted by reason of this impediment.—*De Matrimonio,* II, n. 1211.

[27] There is an instance, however, in which the Vicar Apostolic of Chang-si sought a general sanation for marriages contracted by parties whose mini-

both in relation to the impediment itself and with reference also to the norms established for a radical sanation, there is no reason why it could not be sought if extraordinary circumstances warranted it.

It is stated in canon 1139, § 1, that any marriage entered with a naturally sufficient consent of the parties, but juridically ineffective because of a diriment impediment of ecclesiastical law, or because of a defect of the legally prescribed form, can be radically sanated, provided that the consent has persevered. To the extent, then, that the impediment of nonage is of ecclesiastical law, namely, that it connotes a requirement of the prescribed age of sixteen for the boy and fourteen for the girl over and above the minimum requirement of the natural law which demands a sufficient mental maturity for the giving of a true matrimonial consent, the Church by her common law admits the possibility of the granting of the favor of a radical sanation. If, however, the parties attempted marriage at an age when they did not have sufficient maturity to give a true matrimonial consent, then in so far as the impediment of nonage would in that case really arise from the natural law, and the consent is necessarily defective from the beginning, the Church could not grant a total radical sanation.[28]

Harrigan[29] remarks that although the Church ordinarily does not dispense from the impediment of nonage for the purpose of allowing persons to contract marriage, it dispenses more readily in order that the convalidation of a marriage may be procured. Hence the favor of radical sanation will be granted if the circumstances and reasons attending the petition warrant the use

---

mum age for marriage had been computed in lunar years in place of solar years. The Holy Office responded that no sanation was required. Cf. *supra*, p. 52. The fact that the Vicar Apostolic sought the favor seems to indicate some possibility for the obtaining of it. The reason it was not granted was that it was not required. Cf. *Fontes*, n. 1122; *Collectanea SCPF*, n. 1730.

[28] Cf. canons 1139; 1140.

[29] *The Radical Sanation of Invalid Marriages*, The Catholic University of America Canon Law Studies, n. 116 (Washington, D. C.: The Catholic University of America, 1938), pp. 102; 134–135.

of this extraordinary mode of convalidation. At a later point he suggests what may be considered a grave and sufficient cause, namely the impossibility of warning one or both of the parties of the necessity of renewing their consent, such impossibility arising if there is danger of scandal or of infamy.[30]

Although a radical sanation actually and objectively convalidates the invalid marriage only from the moment the favor is granted, *ex nunc*,[31] nevertheless through a fiction of law by means of an acknowledged retroactivity of status the marriage is considered in its canonical effects as if it had been valid from the beginning, *ex tunc*.[32] But inasmuch as the marriage is actually rendered objectively valid only when radical sanation is granted, it follows that for practical purposes the legitimation of the children is the principal fruit of the retroactive force of the radical sanation.[33]

There is one case which makes this point clear. Canon 1116 states that by the subsequent marriage of the parents, whether their union be real or putative, whether it be newly contracted or convalidated, even if it be only ratified, the offspring becomes legitimate, provided that the parents were able (*habiles*) to contract marriage at the time of the conception, of the pregnancy, or of the birth of this offspring. In relation to this canon the Pontifical Commission of the Authentic Interpretation of the Code was asked: "Whether in virtue of canon 1116 the subsequent marriage of the parents has the effect of legitimating a child begotten by them while they were under the impediment of age or disparity of cult, which impediment, however, had ceased at the time of the marriage." The reply was: "In the negative." [34] Hence in the rare but possible case in which a child should be born before the mother had completed her fourteenth year, or the father his sixteenth year, the child would not be legitimated by

---

[30] *Op. cit.*, p. 109; Gasparri, *De Matrimonio*, II, n. 1229; Cappello, *De Sacramentis*, III, n. 853.

[31] Harrigan, *op. cit.*, p. 43.

[32] Cf. canon 1138; Harrigan, *op. cit.*, p. 9.

[33] Harrigan, *op. cit.*, pp. 49–50.

[34] Dec. 6, 1930- *AAS* XXIII (1931), 25; translation from Bouscaren, *The Canon Law Digest*, I, 550.

the subsequent marriage or simple convalidation of an attempted marriage of the parents. But in such a case, if the parents had attempted marriage or expressed matrimonial consent before their illicit relations so as to make possible a radical sanation, this means of convalidation would also legitimate the child. The radical sanation would convalidate the marriage from the moment the favor was granted, but it would also include, through a fiction of law, a retroactive dispensation from the impediment which in its canonical effects would be considered as extending back to the time when the marriage was first contracted (attempted), and thereby the parties would be considered as if they had enjoyed a status which made them juridically capable (*habiles*) of marriage at that time.[85]

The favor of this extraordinary means of convalidation can be granted only by the Apostolic See.[86] The source of power is found in the person of the Roman Pontiff as the supreme legislator of the universal Church. But the exercise of that power in the normal course of events rests with the various Roman Congregations to which the Holy Father has given jurisdiction.[87] By delegated power, however, issued through the medium of faculties, there are others outside of the Congregations who have the right to grant a radical sanation for a marriage invalidly contracted because of the impediment of nonage. Thus in the faculties usually granted to Apostolic Nuncios and Legates there is contained that of granting a sanation for any marriage invalidly contracted by reason of a diriment impediment of ecclesiastical law, whether public or occult, whether of major or minor degree, with the exception of affinity in the direct line after a marriage has been consummated, of sacred orders and of solemn religious profession. The right to grant the sanation is conditioned on the moral impossibility of a renewal of consent in the ordinary manner and carries with it the obligation of advising the party aware of the impediment of the effect of the sanation. But if the marriage was invalid because of defect of form, a sanation will

[85] Cf. Cappello, *De Sacramentis,* III, 850 bis; Gasparri, *De Matrimonio,* II, n. 1211.

[86] Canon 1141.

[87] Harrigan, *op. cit.,* p. 112.

not be given except in the case in which one of the parties refuses to renew the consent according to the canonical form, or in which grave harm or danger impends for the other party if a celebration in the canonical form is demanded according to the normal requirement of the law.[38]

While the usual faculties granted through the Sacred Congregation of the Propagation of the Faith to the ordinaries in missionary territory exclude the right to grant a sanation for a marriage invalidly contracted because of the impediment of nonage,[39] the usual quinquennial faculties granted to the local ordinaries in the United States through the Sacred Consistorial Congregation include it for use within limited circumstances. Since the specific faculty comes from the Sacred Congregation of the Sacraments, it pertains only to a marriage contracted between two Catholics. It gives the right to sanate radically marriages invalidly contracted because of impediments of ecclesiastical law, whether of major or minor degree, except from the order of priesthood and from affinity in the direct line after a consummated marriage, if there is a great inconvenience of requiring from the party who is ignorant of the nullity of the marriage a

---

[38] Index Facultatum quas, pro locis suae, Nuntiis, Internuntiis et Delegatis Apostolicis penes civitates seu nationes, post Codicis Iuris Canonici publicationem tribuere SSmus Dominus Noster decrevit, ceteris abrogatis. Caput III. Facultates circa matrimonium. . . . n. 31. "Sanandi in radice pro . . . vicibus matrimonia nulla ob impedimentum dirimens, de quo in numero 30 [ab omnibus impedimentis dirimentibus matrimonium, iuris tamen ecclesiastici, sive publicis sive occultis, sive minoris sive maioris gradus, iis tamen exceptis quae ex affinitate in linea recta consummato matrimonio, ex ordine sacro et sollemni professione religiosa proveniunt.], quando moraliter impossibilis est renovatio consensus modo ordinario, monita parte impedimenti conscia de sanationis effectu. Rescriptum vero huiusmodi sanationis in Curia Episcopali diligenter custodiatur, quo omni tempore et eventu de matrimonii validitate et de prolis legitimatione constare possit.

Sed si matrimonium fuerit nullum ob defectum formae, danda non erit sanatio, nisi in casu quo altera pars renuat renovare consensum iuxta formam, aut, si id ab ea exigatur, grave immineat alteri parti malum vel periculum."—cf. Vermeersch-Creusen, *Epitome,* I, n. 872 (Appendix I).

[39] Formulae facultatum quas S.C. de Prop. Fide Ordinariis in terris missionum procurat. (A) Circa Sacramenta et Sacros Ritus: N. 21, 22.—cf. Vermeersch-Creusen, *Epitome,* I, n. 873 (Appendix II).

renewal of consent, provided that the previous matrimonial consent has persevered and there is no danger of a divorce. Moreover the party aware of the impediment is to be advised of the effect of the sanation and a notation of the grant is to be made in the baptismal and marriage registers.[40]

In commenting on these faculties, Harrigan remarks: [41]

> " It appears that the local Ordinaries are empowered to grant sanation only when one party is ignorant of the invalidity of the marriage and the other party is aware of it. Therefore, if both parties are aware of the invalidity or if both parties are ignorant of the invalidity of the marriage, the local Ordinaries apparently cannot grant sanation. It is to be noted, however, that the faculties speak of the party being ignorant of the nullity of the marriage. It does not speak of the party being ignorant of the impediment. For it is not inconceivable for a person to know of the impediment without realizing that it has a diriment effect on the marriage . . . In the second place it is to be particularly noted that the formula of faculties for the Ordinaries restricts their power to cases involving diriment impediments in the strict sense of that term. Therefore, marriages that are invalid solely because of a defect of form do not come within the range of these faculties."

[40] Index facultatum quinquennalium. II. Facultates S. Congr. de disciplina Sacramentorum . . . n. 4: " Sanandi in radice matrimonia nulliter contracta ob aliquod ex impedimentis iuris ecclesiastici maioris vel minoris gradus, exceptis iis provenientibus ex sacro presbyteratus ordine et affinitate in linea recta, matrimonio consummato, si magnum adsit incommodum requirendi a parte, ignara nullitatis matrimonii, renovationem consensus, dummodo tamen prior maritalis consensus perseveret et absit periculum divortii; monita tamen parte conscia impedimenti de effectu huius sanationis et debita facta adnotatione in libro baptizatorum et matrimoniorum."

[41] *Op. cit.*, pp. 157–158.

CHAPTER VI

Judicial Procedure in Declaring the Nullity of a Marriage Arising from Nonage

In the treatment of the judicial procedure to be followed by an ecclesiastical court in declaring null a marriage invalidly contracted because one or both of the parties were impeded by nonage, it is presupposed that the parties followed the prescriptions of canon 1099 and contracted marriage (*species matrimonii*) in the proper canonical form, unless they were legitimately exempted from the form. Thus it is presupposed that the invalidity of the marriage depends solely on the impediment of nonage and not on lack of form, for in the latter case, to declare the parties free would not require a judicial procedure, but an administrative declaration by the ordinary, or by the pastor after consulting the ordinary, without any sort of judicial process or without the intervention of the defender of the bond, would be sufficient.[1]

Certainly marriage cases involving the impediment of nonage will not be of frequent occurrence in diocesan tribunals. A minimum of the required prenuptial investigation by the pastor would readily detect this impediment and prevent the otherwise invalidly contracted marriage. However, deception or inadvertence is not impossible and actual cases of marriages invalidly contracted because of this impediment are not wanting.[2] But

[1] S.C. de Sacramentis, instr., 15 aug. 1936, art. 231—*AAS,* XXVII (1936), 359 (hereafter this Instruction will be referred to as "1936 Instruction"); cf. Marx, *The Declaration of Nullity of Marriages Contracted Outside the Church,* The Catholic University of America Canon Law Studies, n. 182 (Washington, D. C.: The Catholic University of America Press, 1943).

[2] Doheny observes: "It appears that no cases, involving the impediment of age alone, are reported in the volumes of the decisions of the S.R. Rota published to date."—*Canonical Procedure in Matrimonial Cases,* p. 399, note 19. However, he does imply (*ibidem,* p. 402) that such cases are known in diocesan tribunals.

whether cases are real or speculative, there are some particular canonical problems concerning the manner of procedure and the means of proof in the judicial process which cannot be passed over in this treatise.

ARTICLE 1: *The Judicial Process*

The first consideration that presents itself is the manner of judicial procedure. Can matrimonial cases involving the impediment of nonage be decided under the summary and exceptional procedure of canon 1990 and article 226 of the 1936 Instruction, or must such cases be judged within the framework and according to the solemnities of the complete trial? There are some authors who maintain that the enumeration of the seven impediments in canon 1990 is not exhaustive, and that other impediments which can be proved from certain and authentic documents not subject to any contradiction or exception may be included under that canon. Thus Cappello admits that the impediment of nonage may be so included.[3]

In relation to the impediment of nonage, Kay[4] likewise maintains that it could apparently be included under the summary process of canon 1990. He suggests that its omission from the enumeration in the canon is possibly due to the fact that such an event would be rare. But in response to this argument it may be asked whether cases involving the impediments of sacred orders or solemn vows, which are included in the enumeration, would be

[3] *De Sacramentis,* III, n. 891, 7: "Sed praedicta enumeratio non est habenda uti *taxativa.* Nam processus stricte iudicialis tum ratione expensarum tum ob alia incommoda complura, quantum fieri potest, vitandus est. Porro si nullitas matrimonii *evidenter* probari possit etiam praetermissis sollemnitatibus iudicialibus, ita ut fiat locus casui excepto, videtur non esse alienum a mente legislatoris, imo magis esse conforme fini legis et generalibus iuris principiis, ut processus ille omittatur.

Manifestum autem est, praeter septem impedimenta in can. 1900 expresse memorata, alia quoque haberi, quae interdum probari possint 'ex certo et authentico documento, quod nulli contradictioni vel exceptioni obnoxium sit.' Huiusmodi impedimenta sunt aetas . . ."

[4] *Competence in Matrimonial Procedure,* The Catholic University of America Canon Law Studies, n. 53 (Washington, D. C.: The Catholic University of America, 1929), p. 148.

any more frequent? Finally, Kennedy,[5] while favoring the opinion that canon 1990 contains an exhaustive and complete enumeration of impediments and that any extension is contrary to the spirit of the canon, admits that there are some grounds for including other impediments, such as age, legal relationship and public decency, until an official pronouncement is made.

However, the majority of the canonists state that the enumeration in canon 1990 of the impediments which allow the use of the summary process is exhaustive and complete (*taxativa*), and not merely illustrative.[6] But Wernz-Vidal express the opinion that in cases involving the impediment of nonage, since the matter can become evident from an inspection of the parish register, and the absence of a dispensation may be equally evident, the nullity of the marriage can be declared without the solemnities of the ordinary process, or at least that canon 1747 (notorious facts do not need proof) can be applied.[7]

Yet this opinion and position seem to present difficulties. Under the Code and the 1936 Instruction there are only two possible procedures to be followed in deciding cases involving matrimonial impediments (excepting lack of form, which is not strictly an impediment)—the ordinary solemn process, or the summary process in the exceptional cases enumerated in canon 1990. If it is conceded that canon 1990 contains a complete list of the impediments for which the summary process may be employed—and the impediment of nonage is not contained in that enumeration—then that admission seems to force the con-

---

[5] *The Special Matrimonial Process in Cases of Evident Nullity,* The Catholic University of America Canon Law Studies, n. 93 (Washington, D. C.: The Catholic University of America, 1935), pp. 96–97.

[6] Wernz-Vidal, *Ius Matrimoniale,* n. 704; Gasparri, *De Matrimonio,* II, n. 1283; Payen, *De Matrimonio,* III, n. 2721; Vermeersch-Creusen, *Epitome,* III, n. 296; Beste, *Introductio in Codicem,* p. 848; Chelodi, *Ius Matrimoniale,* n. 180.

[7] "Impedimentum aetatis inter casus exceptos non reperitur: videtur dicendum, quod cum sit res, quae adeo potest fieri evidens ex inspectione librorum paroecialium et simili evidentia possit constare de defectu dispensationis obtentae, in tali casu nullitas matrimonii possit declarari eadem ratione sine sollemnitatibus ordinarii processus, aut saltem applicari debet can. 1747." —*op. cit.,* n. 704, nota 57.

clusion that a case involving this impediment must be tried under the ordinary process with all of its solemnities. No alternative is possible. Canon 1990, as Chapter VII of Title XX indicates, contains exceptions to the rules of procedure for matrimonial cases. A law which contains an exception from the law must be strictly interpreted.[8] Even though a specific case involving the impediment of nonage could fit perfectly within the requirements of canon 1990, nevertheless there would be many cases which could not be so included. In view of the general principle of canon law that a law which is enacted as a safeguard against a general danger continues to bind even when in some particular case no danger is present,[9] it seems that there was ample reason for omitting the impediment of nonage from canon 1990 and for making necessary, even in a particular case, the ordinary process.[10]

Moreover, Wernz-Vidal assume that in some cases the impediment of nonage can be proved from an inspection of the parish register (baptismal). As shall be seen, the baptismal record does not offer peremptory proof regarding the listed person's age.[11] Finally, if the fact of nonage was notorious,[12] so as not to need proof, as canon 1747, 1°, indicates, it would not necessarily eliminate the obligation of the solemnities of the process.[13] The means of proof must be considered as something within the process and not as affecting the process itself.

---

[8] Canon 19.

[9] Canon 21.

[10] Cf. Willett, *The Probative Value of Documents in Ecclesiastical Trials*, The Catholic University of America Canon Law Studies, n. 171 (Washington, D. C.: The Catholic University of America Press, 1942), pp. 77–78.

[11] Cf. *infra*, p. 180; Wanenmacher, *Canonical Evidence in Marriage Cases*, n. 9.

[12] Canon 2197, 3°: [Delictum est] *Notorium notorietate facti*, si publice notum sit et in talibus adiunctis commissum, ut nulla tergiversatione celari nulloque iuris suffragio excusari possit.

[13] Noval (*Commentarium Codicis Iuris Canonici*, Lib. IV, *De Processibus* [2 vols., Romae: Marietti, 1920], n. 445): "Ex hoc quod aliqua facta non indigeant probatione non sequitur quod non debeat servari ordo iudiciarius quoad cetera, seu quod praetermitti possint ceteri actus iudiciales praeter probationis, ut puta sententia, citatio ad sententiam, etc." (hereafter cited as *De Processibus*).

Payen,[14] it seems, senses that this opinion of Wernz-Vidal is not entirely satisfactory. He expresses the hope that an authentic declaration of the Holy See will be given, since the matter is of particular use in missionary territory. While not having the force and effect of the awaited declaration, a letter sent by the Apostolic Delegate at Washington to the Bishops of the United States is nevertheless of special importance.[15] The letter contains " some observations which the Sacred Congregation of the Sacraments directed the Apostolic Delegate to address to the Ordinaries on the handling of marriage cases in the United States." [16] It states in part: " The language employed by canon 1990 and article 226 of the Instruction (1936) must be understood and applied exactly in the literal sense without any amplification or extensive interpretations whatsoever. The clear wording of canon 1990 . . . must be understood and interpreted only for the impediments enumerated in this canon without unwarranted extensions. It must be understood that the impediment of age cannot be handled according to the norms of canon 1990, since this impediment is not included in the *taxative* enumeration of the impediments." In view of this letter, diocesan tribunals in the United States have no alternative except to follow the ordinary process in judging marriage cases involving the impediment of nonage. Although privately given for the ordinaries of the United States, it expresses the mind of the Sacred Congregation of the Sacraments and appears to be the only safe course for the ordinaries in other places to follow.

It is not within the scope of this work to give a complete and detailed account of the judicial process to be used by the diocesan tribunal in the deciding of marriage cases which involve the impediment of nonage. Such an account is unnecessary, since it will be the process outlined in the Code and more specifically contained in the 1936 Instruction. It must be emphasized that even though in a particular case the age of the parties may be

[14] *De Matrimonio,* III, n. 2721.

[15] Letter of Apostolic Delegate on Handling of Marriage Cases in the United States, Sept. 23, 1938 (Private)—Bouscaren, *The Canon Law Digest,* II, 531.

[16] *Loc. cit.*

readily determined, leading directly and with the necessary moral certitude to the conclusion that the marriage in question was invalidly contracted, nevertheless that fact does not free the diocesan court from the obligation of employing the formalities of the ordinary process. Proof is only one item in the judicial process. There are other items antecedent and subsequent to the proof itself which pertain to the essence of and are required for the validity of the process. In so far as some of these items have a particular aspect in connection with the impediment under consideration, it will not be without value to give them some consideration.

ARTICLE 2: *The Right to Impugn the Marriage*

Granted that the court has the necessary competence in the case, the first problem will be for the court to ascertain whether the right to impugn the marriage exists, for the collegiate tribunal may not judge or decide any marriage case unless a regular accusation or legally indicted petition has preceded.[17] The right to impugn the marriage belongs exclusively either to the parties themselves or to the promoter of justice, and to no one else. By law, the rights of these persons have restrictions and limitations, which are of importance to note.

A. THE RIGHT OF THE PARTIES

According to canon 1971, § 1, 1°, the consorts in every case of separation or nullity have the right to impugn the marriage, unless they themselves were the cause of the impediment. From the wording of the canon it could seem that the parties in a case involving the impediment of nonage should never be deprived of their right to impugn the marriage; for they could never be the cause of the impediment, which is established by the law itself and completely independent of the will of the parties. Even though they knew of the existence of the impediment and could deceive the priest who witnessed their marriage, or could knowingly neglect to seek a dispensation, they would still not be the cause of the impediment.[18] However, subsequent to the Code, the

---

[17] Canon 1970; 1936 Instruction, art. 34—*AAS*, XXVIII (1936), 321.

[18] Gasparri (*De Matrimonio*, II, n. 1260): "Quod si coniuges scienter

Commission for Interpretation responded *in the negative* to a question presented: " Whether, according to canon 1971, § 1, 1°, the party who was the culpable cause of the impediment or of the nullity of the marriage has also the right to impugn it." [19] In view of this interpretation it may happen that one or both parties of an invalidly contracted marriage on the grounds of nonage may be deprived of their right to impugn it in court. While they could never be the culpable cause of the impediment, they could be the culpable cause of the nullity. Thus if through deceit or fraud one or both of the parties were to falsify their ages, they would be the cause of the nullity of their marriage.

This concept was carried over to the 1936 Instruction.[20] As Doheny observes [21] ". . . it will be helpful to note the nice distinction intended in Article 37, § 1, by the use of the words *sive impedimenti sive nullitatis.* For instance, in question of age a young man might be the inculpable cause of the impediment by the mere fact that he was not sixteen years of age; if he fraudulently and maliciously concealed this fact and married, he would become the culpable cause of the nullity of the marriage in question."

Roberti, however, places a different interpretation on the meaning of the phrase *causa culpabilis sive impedimenti sive nullitatis matrimonii.*[22] It is his opinion that *impedimenti* and *nullitatis* must be understood conjunctively and not disjunctively, that is, the party must be the culpable cause of the impediment *and* of the nullity before he or she (or both) is deprived of the

---

neglexerint dispensationem impetrare ab impedimento ipsis cognito et ideo causam fuerint nullitatis matrimonii? . . . cum agatur de privatione iuris, quae res odiosa est, non videtur posse coniuges privari, hoc in casu, iure accusandi matrimonium."

19 Pont. Cod. Comm., 17 iul. 1933—*AAS,* XXV (1933), 345; translation from Bouscaren, *The Canon Law Digest,* I, 808.

20 Art. 37, § 1. Coniux inhabilis est ad accusandum matrimonium, si fuit causa culpabilis sive impedimenti sive nullitatis matrimonii.

21 *Canonical Procedure in Matrimonial Cases,* p. 89.

22 " De Matrimonii Accusatione "—*Apollinaris,* VI (1933), 441–44. This article was written as *Animadversiones* to the response of the Pontifical Commission of Interpretation, July 17, 1933, cited above. Doheny refers to this article but does not seem to advert to the opinion of Roberti.

right to act as plaintiff in impugning the validity of the marriage. Since the impediment of nonage is independent of the will of the parties contracting,[23] the parties could never be its culpable cause. Roberti bases his argument on the response itself and the confirmation given by the first and third answer.[24] He argues that the use of *sive . . . sive* is a conjunctive (*copulative*) construction. Furthermore, the one who suffers force or fear, and especially the ones who posit a licit and just cause of the impediment, can nevertheless be the cause of the nullity, if they should celebrate the marriage knowing that it was null. Yet in the response such persons are not deprived of their right to impugn the marriage. Hence Roberti concluded that *impedimenti* and *nullitatis* must be taken conjunctively.[25]

Against this opinion of Roberti stand Cappello[26] and Vermeersch-Creusen.[27] It seems difficult to understand how the use of "*sive . . . sive*" demands a conjunctive interpretation, even though the canon together with the responses, because there is

---

[23] Roberti, *loc. cit.*

[24] Pont. Cod. Comm., 17 iul. 1933:

I. An, ad normam canonis 1971 § 1 n. 1, habilis sit ad accusandum matrimonium coniux, qui metum aut coactionem passus sit.

II. An, ad normam eiusdem canonis 1971 § 1 n. 1, habilis sit ad accusandum matrimonium etiam coniux, qui fuerit causa culpabilis sive impedimenti sive nullitatis matrimonii.

III. An causa impedimenti honesta et licita a coniuge apposita obstet quominus coniux ipse habilis sit ad accusandum matrimonium, ad normam canonis 1971 § 1 n. 1.

Resp. Ad I. Affirmative. Ad II. Negative. Ad III. Negative. *AAS,* XXV (1933), 345; *Apollinaris,* VI (1933), 441.

[25] *Loc. cit.*

[26] *De Sacramentis,* III, n. 878, 5: "Verba causa culpabilis *sive impedimenti sive nullitatis matrimonii* . . . sumenda sunt *disjunctive,* non copulative; nam quis potest esse causa culpabilis nullitatis matrimonii, quin fuerit impedimenti . . ."

[27] *Epitome,* III, n. 286, b: "*Causa* autem impedimenti intelligitur causa culpabilis, sive impedimenti, sive nullitatis . . . sc. privatur iure accusandi matrimonium, qui sciens volens actione vel omissione graviter culpabili nullitatem matrimonii directe vel indirecte causavit . . . Iure accusandi matrimonium privabitur ergo qui impedimentum cognoscens illud dolose et cum gravi culpa non manifestavit."

question of the restriction of a right, must be interpreted strictly.[28]

While accepting a disjunctive interpretation, another opinion is expressed by Reh: [29] " The Pontifical Commission, it seems, has used the word ' nullity,' only to indicate that the word ' impediment ' includes vitiated consent, force and fear, etc., i.e., also impediments improperly so called." If this is the meaning of " nullity " in the response (and subsequently in the 1936 Instruction), then it could not include the nullity of a marriage arising from the fact that one of the parties was bound by the diriment impediment of nonage, even though the party was maliciously deceitful in not making known the impediment. The party would not be deprived of his or her right to impugn the marriage.

The latest response from the Pontifical Commission of Interpretation seems to indicate from still another point of view that a person deceitfully hiding a diriment impediment would not be deprived of his right to impugn the marriage.[30] Thus the party must be the direct and guilty party before he loses his right. As Reh points out: [31] " We are quite certain that the word ' directa ' signifies an immediate cause of nullity. Such directness in causality then (we think) would not be true in the case of one who only deceitfully hid the existence of a diriment impediment before marriage. This nullity would be caused directly and immediately by the impediment itself and not directly by the party hiding. Such a person would be a ' causa dolosa ' but ' indirecta ' . . . It is quite true that in such a case one would gain by deceit. But because a specific law was enacted with the

---

[28] Canon 19.

[29] " Guilt of the Plaintiff in a Marriage Case."—*The Jurist,* III (1943), 414, note 11.

[30] Pont. Cod. Comm. 27 iul. 1942, ad III—De Iure Accusandi Matrimonium. D. " Utrum, secundum canonem 1971, § 1, 1o, et responsum diei 17 iulii 1933 ad II, inhabilis ad accusandum matrimonium habendus sit tantum coniux, qui sive impedimenti sive nullitatis matrimonii causa fuit et directa et dolosa, an etiam coniux qui impedimenti vel nullitatis matrimonii causa exstitit vel indirecta vel doli expers." R. "Affirmative ad primam partem, negative ad secundum."—*AAS,* XXXIV (1942), 241. Cf. *The Jurist,* III (1943), 156; Bouscaren, *The Canon Law Digest,* II, 548.

[31] *Art. cit.,* p. 411.

motive of punishing deceit, we cannot conclude that every case in which we find deceit is embraced by it."

It can be seen that the question offers difficulties. However, there seems to be a reason and a foundation for following the opinion suggested by Roberti and Reh and for concluding that Catholic parties who have contracted marriage invalidly because of the impediment of nonage will always have the right to impugn that marriage in their capacity of plaintiffs. Since they can never be the direct and culpable cause of the impediment, since the word "nullity" in the reply of the Pontifical Commission probably does not refer to the nullity that arises from diriment impediments, strictly so called, and especially since the matter must be strictly interpreted, either because it is penal in nature, or because it restricts a right, there appears to be sufficient ground not to deprive them of the right.

This right to impugn the marriage, that is, to act as plaintiff before an ecclesiastical court, belongs only to Catholic parties. Non-Catholics, whether baptized or non-baptized, can never act as plaintiffs unless in each specific case permission is obtained from the Holy Office.[32] As Beste points out,[33] it is most reasonable that the rights and privileges should be denied both to the unbaptized, who by the fact that they are not baptized lack juridical personality in the Church and consequently lack the rights that are conferred with baptism, and to the baptized non-Catholics, who by their lack of faith and subjection have placed an obstacle impeding the bond of union with the Church. The response of the Holy Office makes it clear that it is in view of canon 87 that these persons are deprived of the right. At a later date this Congregation let it be known that apostates from the faith are also included

---

[32] S.C.S. Off., resp., 27 ian. 1928—*AAS,* XX (1928), 75; cf. Bouscaren, *The Canon Law Digest,* I, 762; 1936 Instruction, art. 35 § 3: "Itidem actoris partes agere nequeunt in causis matrimonialibus acatholici sive baptizati sive non baptizati; si quidem autem speciales occurrant rationes ad eosdem admittendos, recurrendum est in singulis casibus ad S.C.S. Officii (cfr. responsionem S.C.S.O., diei 27 ianuarii 1928)."—*AAS.,* XXVIII (1936), 321.

[33] *Introductio in Codicem,* p. 833.

among the non-Catholics who are forbidden to act as plaintiffs in matrimonial cases.[34]

B. The Right of the Promoter of Justice

It is not only the Catholic parties to a marriage invalidly contracted because of the impediment of nonage who can impugn their marriage. The promoter of justice shares with them the cumulative right to act as plaintiff and to impugn the marriage before the ecclesiastical court. According to canon 1971 he has the right when the invalidity of the marriage derives from an impediment that is public by its nature. A response subsequent to the Code indicates that he has this right in virtue of his office,[35] and, as the 1936 Instruction further indicates, by his own right without any previous denunciation made to him by the parties.[36] The one condition postulated for the right of the promoter of justice is that the impediment be public by its nature. On this point, as Doheny remarks,[37] there is an endless discussion and varied opinion, leading to the practical conclusion that there is a real *dubium iuris,* and any well-substantiated opinion may be followed until the matter is settled authoritatively by the Holy See.

It seems to be clear, however, that the Code has intended a distinction between a public impediment, as described in canon 1037, and an impediment public by its nature. As has been developed previously,[38] the only point considered under canon 1037 is whether or not the impediment can be proved in the external forum, irrespective of the nature of the fact on which the impediment depends. So there does not seem to be any justification for interpreting canon 1971, § 1, 2°, in light of the former canon.[39] Gasparri expresses a more commonly accepted view,[40]

---

[34] S.C.S. Off., resp., 11 ian. 1940—*AAS,* XXXII (1940), 52; cf. Bouscaren, *op. cit.,* II, 534.

[35] Pont. Cod. Comm. resp., 17 iul. 1933, ad IV. "An, vi canonis 1971 § 2 promotor iustitiae vi muneris sui agat in iudicio." Resp. Affirmative—*AAS,* XXV (1933), 325; *Apollinaris,* VI (1933), 441.

[36] Art. 35, § 1, 2°—*AAS,* XXVIII (1936), 321.

[37] *Canonical Procedure in Matrimonial Cases,* p. 77.

[38] Cf. *supra,* pp. 72–74.

[39] This is done by Beste, *Introductio in Codicem,* p. 841.

[40] *De Matrimonio,* II, n. 1260: "In impedimentis igitur, quae fundantur

that "public by its nature" refers to those impediments which are founded on facts which are of themselves public, such as the facts that are recorded in public documents.[41] The authorized distinction, then, would be between impediments public by their nature, and those occult by their nature.

Noval,[42] while agreeing that the nature of the fact is the determining note in this regard, considers the possibility of an occult fact becoming public and causing scandal and prejudice to the public good. In such a case he concedes that the promoter of justice has the right to impugn the marriage, since the nature of the matter then demands such action.

An entirely different interpretation of an impediment public by its nature, as used in canon 1971, is given by Wernz-Vidal,[43] one that seems to have become the accepted interpretation by the Sacred Roman Rota.[44] It is to be understood, they contend, in the light of the pre-Code division of impediments into those that are *iuris publici* as distinct from those that are *iuris privati.* The latter are those established principally, although not exclusively, for the private good, while the former are for the common good, the public welfare and the safeguarding of the sanctity of marriage. "Hence, in pre-Code law the right to impugn marriages invalid as a result of impediments *iuris privati* was reserved exclusively to the consorts themselves, whereas any Catholic had the right to impugn the validity of a marriage in cases involving the impediments *iuris publici.*"[45] While the Code has taken away

---

in facto de se publico, ius accusandi matrimonium cumulative competit coniugibus et promotori iustitiae. In aliis vero, quae fundantur in facto de se occulto, ius accusandi solis coniugibus reservatur vel uni eorum, si alter fuerit impedimenti causa."

[41] This opinion is also held by Cappello, *De Sacramentis,* III, n. 878; Coronata, *Institutiones Iuris Canonici,* III, 1486; De Smet, *De Sponsalibus et Matrimonio,* n. 703; Payen, *De Matrimonio,* III, n. 2678.

[42] *De Processibus,* n. 850.

[43] *Ius Matrimoniale,* n. 148.

[44] Cf. S.R. Rota *Nullitas matrimonii,* 11 aug. 1928, *coram R.P.D. Wynen-Sacrae Romanae Rotae Decisiones et Sententiae* (Romae: Typis Polyglottis Vaticanis, 1912–), XX (1928), 402 (hereafter cited *Decisiones*); Doheny, *op. cit.,* pp. 77–80.

[45] Doheny, *op. cit.,* p. 78.

from the faithful, other than the parties themselves, the right to impugn the marriage, it places that right in the hands of the promoter of justice when the common good is involved. It is in this sense, then, according to these authors that impediments public by their nature are to be understood.

But it must be admitted that in regard to the impediment of nonage it is of no great consequence which interpretation is followed. For in either case it must be classed as public. As long as there is a record or witnesses to testify to the date of birth, the age of the parties will be a public fact. On the other hand, certainly the impediment is established for the common good, to safeguard the sanctity of marriage and must be classed as *iuris publici.*

It can be seen that there will be the utmost latitude in bringing a marriage case involving the impediment of nonage before the ecclesiastical court for adjudication. The Catholic parties to the marriage are never deprived of their right, even though they may have deceitfully hidden the impediment when they contracted the marriage. Cumulatively with the parties the promoter of justice will also have the right to impugn the marriage in the capacity of plaintiff.

While it is clear from the Code that neither the parents, relatives nor any other persons enjoy this right,[46] they can denounce the invalid marriage to the ordinary or to the promoter of justice, who can then proceed if the circumstances warrant such action. The 1936 Instruction points out that if the denunciation is made to the ordinary, he should refer the matter to the promoter of justice.[47]

Article 3: *Proofs in the Judicial Process*

At first sight it may seem unnecessary to give any specific treatment concerning the question of proof in the matrimonial process involving the impediment of nonage, for it may appear

[46] Canon 1971, § 2: Reliqui omnes, etsi consanguinei, non habent ius matrimonia accusandi, sed tantummodo nullitatem matrimonii Ordinarii vel promotori iustitiae denuntiandi. Cf. 1936 Instruction, art. 35, § 2.—*AAS,* XXVIII (1936), 321.

[47] Art. 40—*ibid.,* p. 322.

that they can be readily obtained without any particular difficulty. There are, however, certain considerations and cautions which deserve mention. It is obvious that the whole point of the process revolves upon the furnishing of proof regarding the fact that the persons who attempted to contract marriage were juridically incapable of giving a proper matrimonial consent for the reason that one or both of the parties had not attained the requisite canonical age. The sentence of the *officialis* and the two judges on the nullity of the marriage will depend on whether the facts and proofs brought forth in the process give moral certitude that the day of the attempted marriage and the day of birth of one or both of the parties connoted a situation which necessarily implied the presence of the impediment of nonage.

To establish proof of the day on which the marriage took place will ordinarily offer no difficulty. It can be ascertained with certainty from the parish register, which has the value of a public ecclesiastical document.[48] The date on which the marriage occurred seems to be intended as one of the direct objects recorded, in the act of registering the marriage, since it is imposed as an obligation on the pastor or priest who witnessed the marriage to inscribe in the matrimonial register of the parish not only the name of the parties and the witnesses, but also mention of the place and of the day of the celebration of the marriage.[49]

But the equally important consideration of proof, namely, that at the time of the marriage one or both of the parties were not of the requisite age, or, as the fundamental issue will be, proof of the date of birth, may not in some circumstances be so easily obtainable. If an official and authoritative registration of births has been in effect and there is available an official record of the birth of the party involved, it will give the necessary evidence. As Willett observes,[50] "The Code awards the same probative force, in principle, to both civil and ecclesiastical public documents. For, like the latter, civil documents are presumed to be

[48] Canon 1813, § 1, 4o.

[49] Canon 1103, § 1.

[50] *The Probative Value of Documents in Ecclesiastical Trials,* p. 84.

genuine,[51] and therefore prove the facts which are directly and primarily affirmed in them." [52]

It is clear that the purpose of the civil registration of births intends not only to record the fact of birth, but also the date. However, it is hardly to be expected that whenever cases involving the impediment of nonage arise there will always be available accurate and authoritative civil records and a registration of births to afford this necessary information. It seems that the more accustomed thing may be the production of the baptismal record and the inscription of the day of birth on that record as evidence. It is in this regard that definite cautions must be pointed out. The baptismal record does not give full proof of the person's age. Although the inscription in the parochial register has the value of a public ecclesiastical document,[53] it gives full proof only for those items which are directly and primarily affirmed in it,[54] such as the fact of the baptism, the name of the party baptized, the identity of the minister and of the sponsors, and mention of the place and the day of baptism.[55] The date of birth, although it is usually recorded at the same time as a further means of identification, is only accessory information. This does not mean, however, that this information is of no value, but it indicates that it will not afford complete and absolute proof but rather yields only a strong presumption.[56] This presumption, or probable conjecture of an uncertain thing,[57] is not of itself able to overcome the fundamental presumption in every marriage case

[51] Canon 1814.

[52] Canon 1816.

[53] Canon 1813, § 1, 4o.

[54] Canon 1816; cf. Willett, *op. cit.*, p. 75; Wanenmacher, *Canonical Evidence in Marriage Cases*, p. 227.

[55] Canon 777, § 1.

[56] "Scitum est enim libros paroeciales baptizorum, matrimoniorum, funerum, etc., non constituere probationem, nisi quoad factum principale baptismi vel matrimonii; quoad ceteras res aut facta accessoria praedicti libri non constituunt, nisi praesumptionem."—S.R.R. *Nullitas matrimonii*, 23 iul. 1918, *coram R. P. D. Seraphino Many*, dec. X—*Decisiones*, X (1918), 83.

[57] Canon 1825, § 1; 1936 Instruction, art. 170.—*AAS*, XXVIII (1936), 346.

for the validity of the marriage,[58] but when joined with other signs, warrants and indications approximates the value of proof.[59] As Wanenmacher points out,[60] the Sacred Congregation of the Council in a judicial process declared the nullity of a religious profession on the ground of nonage from the evidence of the date of birth set forth in the baptismal register.[61] But in this case there was not the same necessity to overcome the presumption of law which a marriage already contracted possesses.

It can be seen that the statement of Wernz-Vidal [62] that the existence of the impediment of nonage can become evident from an inspection of the parochial books requires some qualification. The baptismal record will certainly give a strong presumption, but that in itself does not seem to be sufficient to enable the judges to declare the marriage null.

Many authors [63] consider the possibility that the fact of nonage can be notorious according to the norms of canon 2197, 3°, and hence regard that fact as a matter which does not require proof.[64] But it is difficult to understand how, under ordinary circumstances, the exact age of a person will be so well known as to be notorious, especially ten or twelve years after the birth has taken place. Perhaps in the case of a prominent family when the birth of a particular child was of some community interest this condition could be verified. But it would be most extraordinary for such a person to contract marriage without a detection of the impediment that prevented the marriage. As infrequent as cases involving the impediment of nonage will be in coming to the ecclesiastical court, it seems that even less frequent will be the situation in which the impediment is so notorious as not to need proof. Moreover, the notoriety of fact does not excuse one from proving

---

[58] Canon 1014; 1936 Instruction, art. 171—*AAS., loc. cit.*

[59] Willett, *op. cit.*, p. 76.

[60] *Canonical Evidence in Marriage Cases*, p. 228.

[61] S.C.C., *Pisauren.*, 28 apr., 16 iun. 1781—*Fontes*, n. 3815; *Thesaurus Resolutionum, S.C.C.* L, 80, 100.

[62] *Ius Matrimoniale*, n. 704, nota 56.

[63] Wernz-Vidal, *loc. cit.;* Gasparri, *De Matrimonio*, II, n. 1283; Vermeersch-Creusen, *Epitome*, III, n. 296; Beste, *Introductio in Codicem*, p. 848.

[64] Canon 1747, 1°.

a case unless the fact be notorious to the judge.[65] Witnesses would have to be introduced to prove the notoriety, hence to prove the fact of nonage at the time of the marriage.

Unless, then, a civil registration of the birth of the person involved has taken place and the record is available to afford full proof of the nonage at the time of the marriage, acceptable witnesses will have to be cited and summoned before the court to substantiate the evidence and the presumption given by the date of birth as recorded in the baptismal record or on the baptismal certificate, and a fortiori to supply the evidence in the event that such a record is not available. While the parents and relatives of the parties are the ones most competent to give the required testimony, and are admissible as witnesses in the matrimonial process,[66] there is always the possibility of suspicion against them, since usually they would not be disinterested parties.[67] It will be the duty of the defender of the bond to propose such objections in his rôle in the process.

In line with the proof of nonage, there must be evidence that a dispensation for the marriage in question was never granted and that the marriage was never convalidated after the impediment ceased. On the former point Doheny observes: [68]

> "In view of cases that have occurred in tribunals, it will not be amiss to warn ecclesiastical authorities to be cautious in declaring null, marriages contracted under the ages demanded by Canon Law. A dispensation may have been duly granted by the proper ecclesiastical authorities. For reasons of prudence the dispensation may have been granted secretly or privately. Hence, diocesan authorities should, as a rule, institute a sedulous search of archives before making any pronouncements in these

---

[65] Wanenmacher, *Canonical Evidence in Marriage Cases*, p. 88.

[66] Canon 1974; 1936 Instruction, art. 122—*AAS*, XXVIII (1936), 338.

[67] Cf. Wanenmacher, *op. cit.*, p. 128. It has been stated as a principle that the testimony of the mother or father as to proof of the age of their child gave only "*semiplena probatio*" when such proof was to the advantage of the child—cf. Mascardus, *Conclusiones Omnium Probationum quae in Utroque Jure Quotidie Versantur* (3 vols., Venetiis, 1593), II, concl. 668, n. 12.

[68] *Canonical Procedure in Matrimonial Cases*, p. 402.

> cases. Examples are not wanting where mistakes might have been easily made if great prudence and dilligent search had not been made."

However, credence must be placed in the absence of any notation on the baptismal and marriage registers. It is presumed that if a dispensation was granted, especially since it would have been unusual, it would also have been noted in the register, and likewise it must be presumed that a notation of the convalidation would have been made in the baptismal record. The appraisal of the lack of evidence for the convalidation would run parallel to the appraisal of a similar lack of evidence in the procedure of declaring a marriage null because of lack of form. Marx has reasonably demonstrated the futility of searching sedulously through the files of all the dioceses in which the parties have lived to investigate the possibility of a validation.[69]

But after using the ordinary means of proof and in following the cautions which prudence dictates, it must be admitted that the case of the nullity of the marriage in question would ordinarily be clear and in view of the evidence the judges would have no great difficulty in arriving at the moral certitude necessary for giving their judgment. This fact, however, does not warrant any abridgement of the remaining formalities of the process—publication of the acts of the process, hearing of the defender of the bond, decree of the conclusion of the case by the presiding judge, discussion of the case by the judge, and finally their sentence. If the sentence is in favor of the nullity of the marriage, then the defender of the bond will have the duty of appealing the case to the court of appeal.[70] It follows from the fact that the ordinary process must be employed that such formalities must also be carried out. No matter how obvious the proof, and no matter how clear the case may be, there does not seem to be any justification for omitting the essential elements of the ordinary matrimonial procedure.

---

[69] *The Declaration of Nullity of Marriages Contracted Outside the Church*, pp. 89–93.

[70] Canon 1986; 1936 Instruction, art. 212, § 2—AAS, XXVIII (1936), 355.

CHAPTER VII

THE CIVIL LAW IMPEDIMENT OF NONAGE IN THE UNITED STATES

THIS concluding chapter may well take the form of an appendix. Civil law can hardly be considered as forming an integral part of a canonical work on marriage, for it is clear in principle that the State is absolutely incompetent to legislate in any way so as to affect the contract of marriage of its baptized subjects, whether they be Catholics or non-Catholics. Its competence is limited to the merely civil effects of marriage, that is, to those effects which are separable from the marriage contract itself.[1]

There are reasons, however, which prompt, and even make necessary, a brief reference to the civil law impediments of nonage insofar as the limitations of the writer allow intrusion into this field. In the first place, civil law impediments have a valid binding force on the unbaptized subjects when they contract marriage between themselves or with a baptized person.[2] The validity or invalidity of such marriages will depend on whether the unbaptized has complied with the prescriptions of the civil law, if it was the intention of the lawmaker that the impediment be of a diriment character. Hence some knowledge of the civil impediment of nonage will be useful. A further reason urging consideration of this matter can be found in canon 1067, § 2. The pastor has an obligation to dissuade youths from contracting marriage before they have attained the age at which, according to the accepted custom of the region, marriage is usually entered. It has bcen suggested that this age will be ordinarily that determined by the civil law, not precisely as civil law, but as reflecting the accepted custom of the locality or State.[3]

---

[1] Cf. canon 1016; Cappello, *De Sacramentis,* III, n. 71.

[2] Cf. *supra,* pp. 33–42.

[3] Cf. *supra,* p. 66.

Before any consideration of the current provisions of each State on the impediment of nonage, it will be of value to view the impediment as it exists in the Common Law.[4] In this legal system, a male at the age of fourteen and a female at the age of twelve can contract a valid marriage.[5] It is concluded that these ages determine the minimum age at which marriage may be contracted, and hence determine a diriment impediment in the canonical sense. The word " concluded " rather than " absolutely certain " must be used because of the indistinct terminology which is employed.[6]

In relation to marriage, the Common Law distinguishes three periods of age: (1) under seven years; (2) from seven years to puberty, that is, fourteen for the boy and twelve for the girl; and (3) over the age of puberty.[7] There is no question that any marriage contracted in the first period is absolutely null, and it is equally certain that a marriage entered in the third period is valid, but a problem arises as to the status of marriages contracted in the second period. Common Law refers to such marriages as "imperfect," "inchoate" or "voidable." However, as Alford points out,[8] the difficulty is one of terminology and not of the objective status of such marriages. Considered in themselves they are invalid, but because they automatically are sanated by the free cohabitation of the parties after they attain the required ages, they are referred to as " imperfect " or " inchoate." If the parties separate or do not live together before attaining the legal age there is clearly no marriage. But the best expression of the

[4] "The common law is that system of unwritten law which grew up in England and forms the basis of the English system." Smith, *A Manual of Elementary Law* (St. Paul, Minn.; West Publishing Co., 1894), p. 47. "The English common law is adopted, so far as suited to American institutions, as the unwritten law of all the States in the United States, except Louisiana."—*Ibid.*, p. 54.

[5] Vernier, *American Family Law*, p. 115; cf. Madden, *A Handbook of the Law of Persons and Domestic Relations* (2. ed., St. Paul, Minn.: West Publishing Co., 1931), p. 28.

[6] Cf. Hannan, "Void and Voidable,"—*The Jurist*, II (1942), 166–170.

[7] Alford, *Jus Matrimoniale Comparatum*, p. 55; cf. Madden, *op. cit.*, p. 28.

[8] *Loc. cit.;* cf. Hannan, *ibid.*, pp. 168–169.

meaning of the Common Law can be found in Blackstone. As he expressed it: [9]

> "This (nonage) is sufficient to avoid all contracts, on account of the imbecility of judgment in the parties contracting. If a boy under fourteen and a girl under twelve marry, the marriage is imperfect and when either party comes of the age of consent, they may disagree and declare the marriage void, without any divorce or sentence in the spiritual [ecclesiastical?] court. This is founded on the civil law. But the canon law pays a greater regard to the constitution than to the age of the parties, for if they are ripe for marriage, it is a good marriage, whatever their age may be. Under our law, if at the age of consent they agree to continue together, they need not be married again. If at the date of the marriage the husband be of lawful age and the wife under twelve, he as well as she may disagree, for in contracts the obligation must be mutual; both must be bound or neither."

In its proper context, it is clear that it is the intent of the Common Law to establish a diriment impediment for all boys below the age of fourteen and all girls below the age of twelve. To the fact that marriages entered below those ages were automatically validated, without the necessity of a renewal of consent, by the continued cohabitation of the parties may be attributed the confusion that has arisen over the status of such marriages. But considered in itself and without this circumstance the "imperfect marriage" was a "null marriage."

The Common Law, however, is no longer the immediate norm in this matter in the vast majority of the States. By statutes they have changed the Common Law rule by providing for higher age limits.[10] It appears that at the present time only five States, namely, Louisiana, Maine, Massachusetts, Mississippi and Rhode Island, have not altered the impediment of nonage as determined by the Common Law. All the remaining States in varying degrees have advanced the legal minimum age at which marriage

[9] *Commentaries on the Law* (edited by B. C. Gavit, Washington, D. C.: Washington Law Book Co., 1941), p. 186.

[10] Vernier, *op. cit.*, p. 115.

may be contracted. But to know with certitude whether it was the intention of the legislature to make the newly established impediment of nonage a diriment impediment in the canonical sense would require a full knowledge of the jurisprudence and the law in each jurisdiction. It can be said that in Delaware nonage is merely an impeding impediment, for the law provides that a defect of age on the part of the parties contracting marriage is a ground for divorce, and not for a declaration of nullity.[11] Similarly in the State of New York it is concluded that the impediment is only impeding.[12] It is Alford's opinion that in all of the other States the impediment of nonage is diriment, irrespective of whether marriages contracted contrary to the law are considered " void " or " voidable." [13]

Many of the States have provision for exceptions. But this does not seem to change the fundamental notion of the impediment itself, for it seems to be the equivalent of granting the competent authority, the judge of the court in most instances, the power to grant a dispensation when circumstances require it, as when the girl is pregnant.

It is important to note that the principle of Common Law for the automatic convalidation of marriage invalidly contracted because of defect of age by the free and voluntary cohabitation of the parties without the necessity of an explicit renewal of consent or a second solemnization of the marriage still remains in force.[14]

As in canon law, the question of parental consent as a requisite for the marriage of minors has become an object of consideration for civil legislation. Similar to canon law, it has no direct effect on the validity of the marriage. As Vernier states: [15] " Modern American statutes without exception now require that minors above their own age of consent, but below a certain age (termed here the 'age of parental consent'), must formally secure the consent of parents or guardians. This does not mean that failure

[11] Cf. Alford, *op. cit.*, p. 374.

[12] Cf. Hammill, "The Impediment of Nonage."—*The Jurist*, III (1943), pp. 475–480.

[13] *Op. cit.*, pp. 57–58.

[14] Alford, *op. cit.*, p. 58.

[15] *American Family Law*, p. 120.

to secure such consent in any way adversely affects the validity of any marriage. Such marriages are in no sense invalid." He further indicates [16] that the only method of enforcing these statutes has been the imposition of penalties upon the persons participating in the contracting of such marriages. Thus if the parties are over the age of consent, yet under the age at which parental consent is necessary, the marriage is none the less valid, even though parental consent has not been obtained.

The following table is appended to afford a summary view of the civil law impediment as it exists in the various States at the present time.[17] But it must be borne in mind that new statutes and modifications are not unusual. If there arises a case which involves an unbaptized person in the civil impediment of nonage, the law as it existed at the time of the (attempted) marriage must be inspected.

	Minimum Age		*Parental Consent*	
State	*Male*	*Female*	*Male*	*Female*
Alabama	17	14	21 [1]	18 [1]
Arizona	18 [2]	16 [2]	21	18
Arkansas	18	16	21	18
California	18 [2]	16 [2]	21 [1]	18 [1]
Colorado	18	18	21	18
Connecticut	16 [2]	16 [2]	21	21
Delaware	18 [2]	16 [2]	21	18
Florida	18 [2]	16 [2]	21	21
Georgia	17	14	— [3]	18
Idaho	18	18	21	18
Illinois	18	16	21	18
Indiana	18	16	21	18
Iowa	16	14	21	18
Kansas	15	12	21	18
Kentucky	16	14	21	21
Louisiana	14	12	21	21
Maine	14	12	21	18
Maryland	18	16	21	18

[16] *Op. cit.*, pp. 126–127.

[17] Adopted from Alford, *op. cit.*, pp. 58–61, and Vernier, *op. cit.*, pp. 116–117, and checked and brought up to date from The Martindale-Hubbell Law Directory (76 annual edition, 2 vols., Summitt, New Jersey: Martindale-Hubbell, Inc.) II.

State	Minimum Age		Parental Consent	
	Male	Female	Male	Female
Massachusetts	14	12	21	18
Michigan	18	16[2]	—[3]	18
Minnesota	18	16	21[1]	18[1]
Mississippi	14	12	21	18
Missouri	15	15	21	18
Montana	18	16	21	18
Nebraska	18	16	21	18
Nevada	18	16	21[1]	18[1]
New Hampshire	14	13	20	18
New Jersey	18	18	21	18
New Mexico	18	16	21	18
New York	16	14	21	18
North Dakota	18	15	21	18
Ohio	18[2]	16[2]	21[1]	21[1]
Oklahoma	18[2]	15[2]	21[1]	18[1]
Oregon	18	15	21	18
Pennsylvania	16[2]	16[2]	21	21
Rhode Island	14	12	21	21
South Carolina	18	14	18	18
South Dakota	18	15	21	18
Tennessee	16	16	18	18
Texas	16	14	21	18
Utah	16	14	21	18
Vermont	16	16	21	18
Virginia	18	16	21	21
Washington	14	15	21	18
West Virginia	18	16	21[1]	21[1]
Wisconsin	18	16	21	18
Wyoming	18	16	21	21
District of Columbia	16	14	21[1]	18[1]

[1] Parental consent is required only for the first marriage.

[2] With the permission of the judge of the competent court marriage can be contracted even below this age.

[3] Parental consent is not required for the male.

CONCLUSIONS

1. The pre-Code impediment of nonage can be traced to Roman Law, requiring puberty for *iustae nuptiae;* to avoid the necessity of physical inspection to ascertain the fact of puberty, Roman Law decreed that the boy was to be considered to have attained puberty upon the completion of his fourteenth year, and the girl upon the completion of her twelfth year.

2. It was made clear in the Decretal period that the determined canonical ages for marriage were established by *praesumptio iuris tantum,* so that if the person had actually attained puberty and had sufficient maturity of mind to give matrimonial consent, he or she could enter a valid marriage before the determined age (*malitia supplet aetatem*).

3. Natural law does not prescribe an impediment of nonage, beyond the requirement of sufficient mental capacity to give matrimonial consent; physical incapacity to use marriage, if due to impuberty, does not prevent the contraction of marriage.

4. Because the impediment of nonage established in the Code of Canon Law is merely ecclesiastical law, it does not bind the unbaptized, nor the Oriental Catholics, nor the Oriental schismatics.

5. It is maintained that the unbaptized are bound by a reasonable and just impediment of nonage established by the competent civil authority, when they contract marriage with the baptized, as well as among themselves.

6. The pre-Code norms for dispensing from the impediment of nonage should not be applied to the present law, nor should it be classified as one which the Church is not wont to dispense.

7. To declare the nullity of a marriage invalidly contracted because of this impediment, the ordinary formal judicial process must be followed, for cases involving this impediment are not included in the inclusive enumeration of canon 1990.

8. Because the impediment is from the law itself and independent of the will of the person, the Catholic party is never deprived of his right to impugn the marriage and act as plaintiff before the ecclesiastical court, even though he deceitfully hid the impediment when contracting the invalid marriage.

BIBLIOGRAPHY

SOURCES

Acta Apostolicis Sedis, Commentarium Officiale, Romae, 1909—.

Acta et Decreta Concilii Plenarii Baltimorensis Tertii, A. D. MDCCCLXXXIV, Baltimorae: John Murphy, 1886.

Acta et Decreta Sacrorum Conciliorum Recentiorum, Collectio Lacensis, 7 vols., Friburgi Brisgoviae: Herder and Co., 1870–1890.

Acta Sanctae Sedis, 41 vols., Romae, 1865–1908.

Bullarium Benedicti XIV *Pont. Opt. Max.,* 3 vols. in 4, Prati, 1845–1847.

Codex Iuris Canonici Pii X Pontificis Maximi iussu digestus Benedicti XV auctoritate promulgatus, Romae: Typis Polyglottis Vaticanis, 1917. Reimpressio, 1933.

Codicis Iuris Canonici Fontes cura Emi Petri Card. Gasparri Editi, 9 vols., Romae: Typis Polyglottis Vaticanis, 1923–1939. (Vol. VII, VIII, IX ed. cura et studio Emi Iustiniani Card. Seredi.)

Collectanea S. Congregationis Propaganda Fide, Romae, 1893.

Collectanea S. Congregationis Propaganda Fide, 2 vols., Romae: Typographia Polyglotta Vaticana, 1907.

Concilii Tridentini Diariorum, Actorum, Epistolarum Tractatuum Nova Collectio, ed. Societas Gorresinana, 13 vols., Friburgi Brisgoviae: B. Herder, 1901—.

Corpus Iuris Canonici, ed. Lipiensis 2., post curas Aemili Ludovici Richteri instruxit Aemilius Friedberg, 2 vols., Lipsiae: Tauchnitz, 1879–1881; ed. anastatice repetita, 2 vols., Lipsiae, 1928.

Corpus Iuris Civilis (Krueger-Momsen-Schoell-Kroll), 3 vols., Berolini: apud Weidmannos, 1928–1929: Vol. I (*Institutiones et Digesta*), ed. stereotype quinta decima, 1929; Vol. II (*Codex Iustinianus*), ed. stereotypa decima, 1929; Vol. III (*Novellae*), ed. stereotypa quinta, 1928.

Decretales D. Gregorii Papae IX, una cum Glossae Restitutae, Romae, 1582.

Decretum Gratiani emendatum et notationibus illustratum una cum glossis Gregorii XIII, Pont. Max. iussu editum, 2 vols., Romae, 1582.

Friedberg, Aemilius, *Quinque Compilationes Antiquae,* Lipsiae, 1882.

Institutes of Gaius and Rules of Ulpian, The, ed. James Muirhead, Edinburg: 19—.

Jaffé, Philippus, *Regesta Pontificum Romanorum a condita Ecclesia ad annum post Christum natum MCXCVIII* (2. ed., Kaltenbrunner, Ewald, Loewenfeld), 2 vols. in 1, Lipsiae, 1885–1888.

Liber Sextus Decretalium D. Bonifatii Papae VIII, suae integritati una cum Clementinis et Extravagantibus, earumque glossis restitutus, Romae, 1582.

Pallottini, S., *Collectio omnium Conclusionum et Resolutionum quae in causis propositis apud Sacrum Congregationem Cardinalium S. Concilii Tridentini interpretum prodierunt et eius institutione anno MCLXIV ad MDCCCLX, distinctis titulis alphabetico ordine per materias digestas,* 18 vols., Romae, 1868–1893.

Potthast, A., *Regista Pontificum Romanorum inde ab anno post Christum natum MCXCVIII ad annum MCCCIV,* 2 vols. in 1, Berolini, 1874–1875.

Sacrae Romanae Rotae Decisiones seu Sententiae . . . quae prodierunt anno 1909–1932, 24 vols., Romae: Typis Vaticanis, 1912–1940.

Thesaurus Resolutionum Sacrae Congregationis Concilii, 167 vols., Romae, 1718–1908.

REFERENCE WORKS

Alford, Culver, *Jus Matrimoniale Comparatum,* New York: P. J. Kenedy & Sons, 1938.

Altimarus, Blasius, *Tractus de Nullitate,* 2 vols., Neapoli, 1678.

Antonelli, Joseph, *Medicina Pastoralis in Usum Confessorum et Curiarum Ecclesiasticarum,* 3. ed., 3 vols., Romae, 1909.

Ayrinhac, Henry-Lydon, Patrick J., *Marriage Legislation in the New Code of Canon Law,* new, revised ed., New York: Benziger Brothers, 1938.

Barbosa, Augustinus, *Pastoralis Sollicitudinis, sive De Officio et Potestate Episcopi Descriptio,* Lugduni, 1656.

Bernardus, Papiensis, *Summa Decretalium,* ed. E. A. T. Laspeyres, Ratisbonae, 1861.

Beste, Ubaldus, *Introductio in Codicem,* Collegeville, Minn.: St. John's Abbey Press, 1938.

Blackstone, *Commentaries on the Law,* edited by B. C. Gavit, Washington, D. C.: Washington Law Book Co., 1941.

Bouscaren, T. Lincoln, *The Canon Law Digest,* 2 vols., Milwaukee: The Bruce Publishing Co., 1934–1943.

Brooks, Fowler, *The Psychology of Adolescence,* Boston: Houghton Mifflin Co., 1929.

Cappello, Felix, *Tractus Canonico-Moralis de Sacramentis,* 3 vols. in 6, Vol. III, *De Matrimonio,* ed. quarta emendata et aucta, Romae, Taurinorum Augustae: Officina Libraria Marietti, 1939.

Chelodi, Ioannes, *Ius Matrimoniale iuxta Codicem Iuris Canonici,* 3. ed., Trento: Libreria Moderna Editrice A. Ardesi et C., 1921.

Cicognani, Amleto, *Canon Law,* 2. revised ed., authorized English version by Joseph O'Hara and Francis Brennan, Philadelphia: The Dolphin Press, 1935.

Coronata, Matthaeus, *Institutiones Iuris Canonici,* 5 vols., Taurini: Marietti, 1933–1939; Vols. I–II, 2 ed., 1939; Vol. III, 1933; Vol. IV, 1935; Vol. V, 1936.

Cronin, Michael, *The Science of Ethics,* 2 vols., Dublin: H. M. Gill, 1922.

D'Annibale, Joseph, *Summula Theologicae Moralis,* 5. ed., 3 vols., Romae, 1908.

De Becker, Iulius, *De Matrimonio Praelectiones Canonicae,* 2. ed., Louvain: Fr. Ceutrick, 1931.

De Justis, Vincentius, *De Dispensationibus Matrimonialibus,* Lucae, 1726.

De Smet, A., *Tractatus Theologico-Canonicus De Sponsalibus et Matrimonio,* ed. quarta (inde a Codice altera), Brugis: Car. Beyaert, 1927.

Dillon, Robert, *Common Law Marriage,* The Catholic University of America Canon Law Studies, n. 153, Washington, D. C.: The Catholic University of America Press, 1942.

Doheny, William J., *Canonical Procedure in Matrimonial Cases,* Milwaukee: The Bruce Publishing Co., 1938.

Donovan, James, *The Pastor's Obligation in Pre-nuptial Investigation,* The Catholic University of America Canon Law Studies, n. 115, Washington, D. C.: The Catholic University of America, 1938.

Dubé, Arthur, *The General Principles for the Reckoning of Time in Canon Law,* The Catholic University of America Canon Law Studies, n. 144, Washington, D. C.: The Catholic University of America Press, 1941.

Eschbach, Alphonse, *Disputationes Physiologico-Theologicae,* Romae: Desclée, Lefebure et Socii, 1901.

Fagnanus, Prosper, *Commentaria in Quinque Libros Decretalium,* 5 vols. in 3, Venetiis, 1661.

Feije, Henricus, *De Impedimentis et Dispensationibus Matrimonialibus,* 3. ed., Lovanii, 1885.

Gasparri, Petrus, *Tractatus Canonicus de Matrimoni,* ed. nova ad mentem Codicis I. C., 2 vols., Romae: Typis Polyglottis Vaticanis, 1932; also, ed. tertia, Parisiis, 1904.

Harrigan, Robert, *The Radical Sanation of Invalid Marriages,* The Catholic University of America Canon Law Studies, n. 116, Washington, D. C.: The Catholic University of America, 1938.

Hostiensis (Henricus de Segusia), *In Quinque Libros Decretalium Commentaria,* 5 vols. in 3, Venetiis, 1581.

Joyce, George, *Christian Marriage* (Heythrop Series: I) London and New York: Sheed and Ward, 1933.

Kay, Thomas, *Competence in Matrimonial Procedure,* The Catholic University of America Canon Law Studies, n. 53, Washington, D. C.: The Catholic University of America, 1929.

Kennedy, Edwin, *The Special Matrimonial Process in Cases of Evident Nullity,* The Catholic University of America Canon Law Studies, n. 93, Washington, D. C.: The Catholic University of America, 1935.

Leurenius, Petrus, *Forum Ecclesiasticum in quo Ius Canonicum Universum Explicatur,* 5 vols. in 3, Venetiis, 1729.

Liberatore, M., *Institutiones Philosophicae,* vol. III, *Ethica et Ius Naturae,* 8. ed., Romae, 1855.

Madden, J. W., *A Handbook of the Law of Persons and Domestic Relations,* 2. ed., St. Paul, Minn.: West Publishing Co., 1931.

Moroto, Philippus, *Institutiones Iuris Canonici ad normam Novi Codicis,* 2 vols., Vol. I, 3. ed., Romae: apud Commentarium pro Religiosis, 1921.

Martindale-Hubbell, *The Martindale-Hubbell Law Directory,* 2 vols., 76. annual ed., Summitt, New Jersey: Martindale-Hubbell, Inc., 1944.

Marx, Adolph, *The Declaration of Nullity of Marriages Contracted Outside the Church,* The Catholic University of America Canon Law Studies, n. 182, Washington, D. C.: The Catholic University of America Press, 1943.

Mascardus, I., *Conclusiones Omnium Probationum quae in Utroque Iure Quotidie Versantur,* 3 vols., Venetiis, 1593.

McCloskey, J., *The Subject of Ecclesiastical Law According to Canon 12,* The Catholic University of America Canon Law Studies, n. 165, Washington, D. C.: The Catholic University of America Press, 1942.

Noval, Joseph, *Commentarium Codicis Iuris Canonici,* Lib. IV, *De Processibus,* 2 vols., Romae: Marietti, 1920–1932.

Ottaviani, Alaphridus, *Institutiones Iuris Publici Ecclesiastici,* ed. altera, 2 vols., Civitate Vaticana: Typis Polyglottis Vaticanis, 1935–1936.

Payen, G., *De Matrimonio in Missionibus ac Potissimum in Sinis Tractatus Practicus et Casus,* 2. ed., 3 vols., Zi-ka-wei: In T'ou-sè-wè, 1935–1936.

Perrone, Ioannes, *De Matrimonio Christiano,* 3 vols., Romae, 1858.

Pey, Jean, *De l'autorité des deux puissances,* 4 vols., Strasbourg, 1788.

Pirhing, Ernricus, *Jus Canonicum in Quinque Libros Decretalium Distributum Nova Methodo Explicatum,* ed. novissima, 5 vols. in 4, Dilingae, 1722.

Pyrrhus, Corradus, *Praxis Dispensationum Apostolicarum et Solidissimo Romae Curiae Stylo,* Venetiis, 1735.

Quigley, Joseph, *A Summary of the Canon Law on Matrimonial Impediments and Dispensations,* 2. ed., Philadelphia: The Dolphin Press, 1942.

Reiffenstuel, Anacletus, *Ius Canonicum Universum,* 5 vols. in 7, Parisiis, 1864–1870.

Richmond, M.–Hall, F., *Child Marriages,* New York: The Russell Sage Foundation, 1925.

———, *Marriage and the State,* New York; The Russell-Sage Foundation, 1929.

Sanchez, Thomas, *Disputationum de Sancto Matrimonii Sacramento Tomi Tres,* Antverpiae, 1626.

Schmalzgrueber, Franciscus, *Ius Ecclesiasticum Universum,* 5 vols. in 12, Romae, 1843–1845.

Schumacher, Henry, M. D., *The Adolescent, His Development and His Major Problem,* Washington, D. C.: The Catholic Conference on Family Life, 1938.

Smith, Walter D., *A Manual of Elementary Law,* St. Paul, Minn.: West Publishing Co., 1894.

Tanquerey, Ad., *Synopsis Theologicae Moralis et Pastoralis,* 3 vols., Vol 1, ed. duodecima, 1936; Vol. II, ed. nona, 1931; Vol. III, ed. decima, 1937, Parisiis-Desclée et Socii.

Vermeersch, A.–Creusen, J., *Epitome Iuris Canonici,* 3 vols., Vol. I, ed. sexta, 1937, Vol. II, ed. quinta, 1936, Vol. III, ed. quinta, 1936, Mechliniae—Romae: H. Dessain.

Vernier, Chester, *American Family Laws,* 2 vols., Stanford University, California: The Stanford University Press, 1931–1932.

Vlaming, Th. M., *Praelectiones Iuris Matrimonii,* 3. ed., 2 vols. Bussum in Hollandia, Vol. I, 1919, Vol. II, 1921.

Wanenmacher, Francis, *Canonical Evidence in Marriage Cases,* The Catholic University of America Canon Law Studies, n. 9, Philadelphia: Dolphin Press, 1935.

Wernz, Franciscus, *Ius Decretalium,* 6 vols., Romae et Prati, 1898–1905, Vol. IV, *Ius Matrimoniale Ecclesiae Catholicae,* 1904.

Wernz, Franciscus–Vidal, Petrus, *Ius Canonicum,* 7 vols. in 8, Romae: apud Aedes Universitatis Gregorianae, 1923–1938, Vol. V, *Ius Matrimoniale,* 2. ed., 1928.

Willett, Robert, *The Probative Value of Documents in Ecclesiastical Trials,* The Catholic University of America Canon Law Studies, n. 171, Washington, D. C.: The Catholic University of America Press, 1942.

ARTICLES

Cappello, F., "Jus Ecclesiae Latinae cum Jure Ecclesiae Orientalis Comparatum."—*Jus Pontificum,* VII (1927), 55–71.

Dalpiaz, V., "An Orientales Schismatici legibus matrimonialibus Ecclesiae latinae teneantur?"—*Apollinaris,* X (1937), 457–459.

Hammill, J., "The Impediment of Nonage."—*The Jurist,* III (1943), 475–480.

Hannan, J., "Void and Voidable."—*The Jurist,* II (1942), 166–170.

Heneghan, J., "The Decree 'Tametsi' in the United States."—*The Jurist,* III (1943), 318–326.

Heneghan, J., "Civil Marriage License."—*The Jurist,* III (1943), 310–318.

Herman, A., "Regunturne Orientales dissidentes legibus matrimonialibus Ecclesiae latinae?"—*Periodica de Re Morali, Canonica, Liturgica,* XXVII (1938), 7–20.

Onclin, W., "De Regimine Matrimonii Fidelem et inter Infidelem."—*Ephemerides Theologicae Lovanienses,* X (1933), 47–62.

Reh, F., "Guilt of the Plaintiff in a Marriage Case."—*The Jurist,* III (1943), 404–412.

Roberti, F., "De Matrimonii Accusatione."—*Apollinaris,* VI (1933), 441–444.

PERIODICALS

Analecta Iuris Pontificii, Romae, 1855–1868; Parisiis, 1869–1891.

Apollinaris, Romae, 1928–

Ecclesiastical Review, The American, Philadelphia, 1889–1943; Baltimore, 1944–

Ephemerides Theologicae Lovanienses, Lovanii, Universitas Catholica Lovaniensis, 1924–

Jurist, The, Washington, D. C., 1941–

Jus Pontificium, Romae, 1921–

Periodica de Re Canonica et Morali utilia praesehtim Religiosis et Missionariis Brugis, 1905–; from the year 1927: *Periodica de Re Canonica, Morali, Liturgica.*

ABBREVIATIONS

AAS—Acta Apostolicae Sedis.

ASS—Acta Sanctae Sedis.

C.—Codex Iustinianus.

D.—Digesta Iustinianus.

Collectanea SCPF.—Collectanea S. C. de Propaganda Fide.

Coll. Lac.—Collectio Lacensis.

Fontes—Codicis Iuris Canonici Fontes cura . . . Gasparri editi.

Inst.—Institutiones Iustinianae.

Pont. Cod. Comm.—Pontificia Commissio ad Codicis Canones authentica Interpretandas.

S.C.C.—Sacra Congregatio Concilii.

S.C.P.F.—Sacra Congregatio de Propaganda Fide.

S.C.S. Off.—Sacra Congregatio Sancti Officii.

S.R.R.—Sacra Romana Rota.

INDEX

BIOGRAPHICAL NOTE

John Coyle O'Dea was born in San Francisco, California, on October 24, 1913. After completing his grammar school education in Star of the Sea School, he entered St. Ignatius High School and graduated in 1931. That same year he entered St. Joseph's College, Mountain View, California, the preparatory seminary for the Archdiocese of San Francisco. In 1934 he entered St. Patrick's Seminary, Menlo Park, California, and with the completion of his philosophy course received the degree of Bachelor of Arts. He was ordained to the Sacred Priesthood at St. Mary's Cathedral, San Francisco, on May 18, 1940. After a year of parochial work in San Francisco he was assigned to the Catholic University of America to pursue a course of studies in the School of Canon Law. He received the Baccalaureate Degree in Canon Law in May, 1942, and the Licentiate Degree in Canon Law in May, 1943.

CANON LAW STUDIES*

1. FRERIKS, REV. CELESTINE A., C.PP.S., J.C.D., Religious Congregations in Their External Relations, 121 pp., 1916.
2. GALLIHER, REV. DANIEL M., O.P., J.C.D., Canonical Elections, 117 pp., 1917.
3. BORKOWSKI, REV. AURELIUS L., O.F.M., J.C.D., De Confraternitatibus Ecclesiasticis, 136 pp., 1918.
4. CASTILLO, REV. CAYO, J.C.D., Disertacion Historico-Canonica sobre la Potestad del Cabildo en Sede Vacante o Impedida del Vicario Capitular, 99 pp., 1919 (1918).
5. KUBELBECK, REV. WILLIAM J., S.T.B., J.C.D., The Sacred Penitentiaria and Its Relation to Faculties of Ordinaries and Priests, 129 pp., 1918.
6. PETROVITS, REV. JOSEPH, J. C., S.T.D., J.C.D., The New Church Law on Matrimony, X-461 pp., 1919.
7. HICKEY, REV. JOHN J., S.T.B., J.C.D., Irregularities and Simple Impediments in the New Code of Canon Law, 100 pp., 1920.
8. KLEKOTKA, REV. PETER J., S.T.B., J.C.D., Diocesan Consultors, 179 pp., 1920.
9. WANENMACHER, REV. FRANCIS, J.C.D., The Evidence in Ecclesiastical Procedure Affecting the Marriage Bond, 1920 (Printed 1935).
10. GOLDEN, REV. HENRY FRANCIS, J.C.D., Parochial Benefices in the New Code, IV-119 pp., 1921 (Printed 1925).
11. KOUDELKA, REV. CHARLES J., J.C.D., Pastors, Their Rights and Duties According to the New Code of Canon Law, 211 pp., 1921.
12. MELO, REV. ANTONIUS, O.F.M., J.C.D., De Exemptione Regularium, X-188 pp., 1921.
13. SCHAAF, REV. VALENTINE THEODORE, O.F.M., S.T.B., J.C.D., The Cloister, X-180 pp., 1921.
14. BURKE, REV. THOMAS JOSEPH, S.T.D., J.C.D., Competence in Ecclesiastical Tribunals, IV-117 pp., 1922.
15. LEECH, REV. GEORGE LEO, J.C.D., A Comparative Study of the Constitution "Apostolicae Sedis" and the "Codex Juris Canonici," 179 pp., 1922.
16. MOTRY, REV. HUBERT LOUIS, S.T.D., J.C.D., Diocesan Faculties According to the Code of Canon Law, II-167 pp., 1922.
17. MURPHY, REV. GEORGE LAWRENCE, J.C.D., Delinquencies and Penalties in the Administration and the Reception of the Sacraments, IV-121 pp., 1923.

* Below n. 100 only the following numbers are still available: Nn. 3, 4, 9, 25, 34, 57 and 75. Beginning with n. 100 only the following are unavailable: Nn. 100-111 inclusive, and n. 113.

18. O'Reilly, Rev. John Anthony, S.T.B., J.C.D., Ecclesiastical Sepulture in the New Code of Canon Law, II-129 pp., 1923.
19. Michalicka, Rev. Wenceslas Cyril, O.S.B., J.C.D., Judicial Procedure in Dismissal of Clerical Exempt Religious, 107 pp., 1923.
20. Dargin, Rev. Edward Vincent, S.T.B., J.C.D., Reserved Cases According to the Code of Canon Law, IV-103 pp., 1924.
21. Godfrey, Rev. John A., S.T.B., J.C.D., The Right of Patronage According to the Code of Canon Law, 153 pp., 1924.
22. Hagedorn, Rev. Francis Edward, J.C.D., General Legislation on Indulgences, II-154 pp., 1924.
23. King, Rev. James Ignatius, J.C.D., The Administration of the Sacraments to Dying Non-Catholics, V-141 pp., 1924.
24. Winslow, Rev. Francis Joseph, O.F.M., J.C.D., Vicars and Prefects Apostolic, IV-149 pp., 1924.
25. Correa, Rev. Jose Servelion, S.T.L., J.C.D., La Potestad Legislativa de la Iglesia Catolica, IV-127 pp., 1925.
26. Dugan, Rev. Henry Francis, A.M., J.C.D., The Judiciary Department of the Diocesan Curia, 87 pp., 1925.
27. Keller, Rev. Charles Frederick, S.T.B., J.C.D., Mass Stipends, 167 pp., 1925.
28. Paschang, Rev. John Linus, J.C.D., The Sacramentals According to the Code of Canon Law, 129 pp., 1925.
29. Piontek, Rev. Cyrillus, O.F.M., S.T.B., J.C.D., De Indulto Exclaustrationis necnon Saecularizationis, XIII-289 pp., 1925.
30. Kearney, Rev. Richard Joseph, S.T.B., J.C.D., Sponsors at Baptism According to the Code of Canon Law, IV-127 pp., 1925.
31. Bartlett, Rev. Chester Joseph, A.M., LL.B., J.C.D., The Tenure of Parochial Property in the United States of America, V-108 pp., 1926.
32. Kilker, Rev. Adrian Jerome, J.C.D., Extreme Unction, V-425 pp., 1926.
33. McCormick, Rev. Robert Emmett, J.C.D., Confessors of Religious, VIII-266 pp., 1926.
34. Miller, Rev. Newton Thomas, J.C.D., Founded Masses According to the Code of Canon Law, VII-93 pp., 1926.
35. Roelker, Rev. Edward G., S.T.D., J.C.D., Principles of Privilege According to the Code of Canon Law, XI-166 pp., 1926.
36. Bakalarczyk, Rev. Richardus, M.I.C., J.U.D., De Novitiatu, VIII-208 pp., 1927.
37. Pizzuti, Rev. Lawrence, O.F.M., J.U.L., De Parochis Religiosis, 1927. (Not Printed.)
38. Bliley, Rev. Nicholas Martin, O.S.B., J.C.D., Altars According to the Code of Canon Law, XIX-132 pp., 1927.
39. Brown, Mr. Brendan Francis, A.B., LL.M., J.U.D., The Canonical Juristic Personality with Special Reference to its Status in the United States of America, V-212 pp., 1927.

40. Cavanaugh, Rev. William Thomas, C.P., J.U.D., The Reservation of the Blessed Sacrament, VIII-101 pp., 1927.
41. Doheny, Rev. William J., C.S.C., A.B., J.U.D., Church Property: Modes of Acquisition, X-118 pp., 1927.
42. Feldhaus, Rev. Aloysius H., C.PP.S., J.C.D., Oratories, IX-141 pp., 1927.
43. Kelly, Rev. James Patrick, A.B., J.C.D., The Jurisdiction of the Simple Confessor, X-208 pp., 1927.
44. Neuberger, Rev. Nicholas J., J.C.D., Canon 6 or the Relation of the Codex Juris Canonici to the Preceding Legislation, V-95 pp., 1927.
45. O'Keefe, Rev. Gerald Michael, J.C.D., Matrimonial Dispensations, Powers of Bishops, Priests, and Confessors, VIII-232 pp., 1927.
46. Quigley, Rev. Joseph A. M., A.B., J.C.D., Condemned Societies, 139 pp., 1927.
47. Zaplotnik, Rev. Johannes Leo, J.C.D., De Vicariis Foraneis, X-142 pp., 1927.
48. Duskie, Rev. John Aloysius, A.B., J.C.D., The Canonical Status of the Orientals in the United States, VIII-196 pp., 1928.
49. Hyland, Rev. Francis Edward, J.C.D., Excommunication, Its Nature, Historical Development and Effects, VIII-181 pp., 1928.
50. Reinmann, Rev. Gerald Joseph, O.M.C., J.C.D., The Third Order Secular of Saint Francis, 201 pp., 1928.
51. Schenk, Rev. Francis J., J.C.D., The Matrimonial Impediments of Mixed Religion and Disparity of Cult, XVI-318 pp., 1929.
52. Coady, Rev. John Joseph, S.T.D., J.U.D., A.M., The Appointment of Pastors, VIII-150 pp., 1929.
53. Kay, Rev. Thomas Henry, J.C.D., Competence in Matrimonial Procedure, VIII-164 pp., 1929.
54. Turner, Rev. Sidney Joseph, C.P., J.U.D., The Vow of Poverty, XLIX-217 pp., 1929.
55. Kearney, Rev. Raymond A., A.B., S.T.D., J.C.D., The Principles of Delegation, VII-149 pp., 1929.
56. Conran, Rev. Edward James, A.B., J.C.D., The Interdict, V-163 pp., 1930.
57. O'Neill, Rev. William H., J.C.D., Papal Rescripts of Favor, VII-218 pp., 1930.
58. Bastnagel, Rev. Clement Vincent, J.U.D., The Appointment of Parochial Adjutants and Assistants, XV-257 pp., 1930.
59. Ferry, Rev. William A., A.B., J.C.D., Stole Fees, V-136 pp., 1930.
60. Costello, Rev. John Michael, A.B., J.C.D., Domicile and Quasi-Domicile, VII-201 pp., 1930.
61. Kremer, Rev. Michael Nicholas, A.B., S.T.B., J.C.D., Church Support in the United States, VI-136 pp., 1930.
62. Angulo, Rev. Luis, C.M., J.C.D., Legislation de la Iglesia sobre la intencion en la application de la Santa Misa, VII-104 pp., 1931.

63. Frey, Rev. Wolfgang Norbert, O.S.B., A.B., J.C.D., The Act of Religious Profession, VIII-174 pp., 1931.
64. Roberts, Rev. James Brendan, A.B., J.C.D., The Banns of Marriage, XIV-140 pp., 1931.
65. Ryder, Rev. Raymond Aloysius, A.B., J.C.D., Simony, IX-151 pp., 1931.
66. Campagna, Rev. Angelo, Ph.D., J.U.D., Il Vicario Generale del Vescovo, VII-205 pp., 1931.
67. Cox, Rev. Joseph Godfrey, A.B., J.C.D., The Administration of Seminaries, VI-124 pp., 1931.
68. Gregory, Rev. Donald J., J.U.D., The Pauline Privilege, XV-165 pp., 1931.
69. Donohue, Rev. John F., J.C.D., The Impediment of Crime, VII-110 pp., 1931.
70. Dooley, Rev. Eugene A., O.M.I., J.C.D., Church Law on Sacred Relics, IX-143 pp., 1931.
71. Orth, Rev. Clement Raymond, O.M.C., J.C.D., The Approbation of Religious Institutes, 171 pp., 1931.
72. Pernicone, Rev. Joseph M., A.B., J.C.D., The Ecclesiastical Prohibition of Books, XII-267 pp., 1932.
73. Clinton, Rev. Connell, A.B., J.C.D., The Paschal Precept, IX-108 pp., 1932.
74. Donnelly, Rev. Francis B., A.M., S.T.L., J.C.D., The Diocesan Synod, VIII-125 pp., 1932.
75. Torrente, Rev. Camilo, C.M.F., J.C.D., Las Procesiones Sagradas, V-145 pp., 1932.
76. Murphy, Rev. Edwin J., C.PP.S., J.C.D., Suspension Ex Informata Conscientia, XI-122 pp., 1932.
77. MacKenzie, Rev. Eric F., A.M., S.T.L., J.C.D., The Delict of Heresy in its Commission, Penalization, Absolution, VII-124 pp., 1932.
78. Lyons, Rev. Avitus E., S.T.B., J.C.D., The Collegiate Tribunal of First Instance, XI-147 pp., 1932.
79. Connolly, Rev. Thomas A., J.C.D., Appeals, XI-195 pp., 1932.
80. Sangmeister, Rev. Joseph V., A.B., J.C.D., Force and Fear as Precluding Matrimonial Consent, V-211 pp., 1932.
81. Jaeger, Rev. Leo A., A.B., J.C.D., The Administration of Vacant and Quasi-Vacant Episcopal Sees in the United States, IX-229 pp., 1932.
82. Rimlinger, Rev. Herbert T., J.C.D., Error Invalidating Matrimonial Consent, VII-79 pp., 1932.
83. Barrett, Rev. John D. M., S.S., J.C.D., A Comparative Study of the Third Plenary Council of Baltimore and the Code, IX-221 pp., 1932.
84. Carberry, Rev. John J., Ph.D., S.T.D., J.C.D., The Juridical Form of Marriage, X-177 pp., 1934.
85. Dolan, Rev. John L., A.B., J.C.D., The Defensor Vinculi, XII-157 pp., 1934.

86. HANNAN, REV. JEROME D., A.M., S.T.D., LL.B., J.C.D., The Canon Law of Wills, IX-517 pp., 1934.
87. LEMIEUX, REV. DELISE A., A.M., J.C.D., The Sentence in Ecclesiastical Procedure, IX-131 pp., 1934.
88. O'ROURKE, REV. JAMES J., A.B., J.C.D., Parish Registers, VII-109 pp., 1934.
89. TIMLIN, REV. BARTHOLOMEW, O.F.M., A.M., J.C.D., Conditional Matrimonial Consent, X-381 pp., 1934.
90. WAHL, REV. FRANCIS X., A.B., J.C.D., The Matrimonial Impediments of Consanguinity and Affinity, VI-125 pp., 1934.
91. WHITE, REV. ROBERT J., A.B., LL.B., S.T.B., J.C.D., Canonical Ante-Nuptial Promises and the Civil Law, VI-152 pp., 1934.
92. HERRERA, REV. ANTONIO PARRA, O.C.D., J.C.D., Legislacion Ecclesiastica sobra el Ayuno y la Abstinencia, XI-191 pp., 1935.
93. KENNEDY, REV. EDWIN J., J.C.D., The Special Matrimonial Process in Cases of Evident Nullity, X-165 pp., 1935.
94. MANNING, REV. JOHN J., A.B., J.C.D., Presumption of Law in Matrimonial Procedure, XI-111 pp., 1935.
95. MOEDER, REV. JOHN M., J.C.D., The Proper Bishop for Ordination and Dimissorial Letters, VII-135 pp., 1935.
96. O'MARA, REV. WILLIAM A., A.B., J.C.D., Canonical Causes for Matrimonial Dispensations, IX-155 pp., 1935.
97. REILLY, REV. PETER, J.C.D., Residence of Pastors, IX-81 pp., 1935.
98. SMITH, REV. MARINER T., O.P., S.T.Lr., J.C.D., The Penal Law for Religious, VII-169 pp., 1935.
99. WHALEN, REV. DONALD W., A.M., J.C.D., The Value of Testimonial Evidence in Matrimonial Procedure, XIII-297 pp., 1935.
100. CLEARY, REV. JOSEPH F., J.C.D., Canonical Limitations on the Alienation of Church Property, VIII-141 pp., 1936.
101. GLYNN, REV. JOHN C., J.C.D., The Promoter of Justice, XX-337 pp., 1936.
102. BRENNAN, REV. JAMES H., S.S., M.A., S.T.B., J.C.D., The Simple Convalidation of Marriage, VI-135 pp., 1937.
103. BRUNINI, REV. JOSEPH BERNARD, J.C.D., The Clerical Obligations of Canons 139 and 142, X-121 pp., 1937.
104. CONNOR, REV. MAURICE, A.B., J.C.D., The Administrative Removal of Pastors, VIII-159 pp., 1937.
105. GUILFOYLE, REV. MERLIN JOSEPH, J.C.D., Custom, XI-144 pp., 1937.
106. HUGHES, REV. JAMES AUSTIN, A.B., A.M., J.C.D., Witnesses in Criminal Trials of Clerics, IX-140 pp., 1937.
107. JANSEN, REV. RAYMOND J., A.B., S.T.L., J.C.D., Canonical Provisions for Catechetical Instruction, VII-153 pp., 1937.
108. KEALY, REV. JOHN JAMES, A.B., J.C.D., The Introductory Libellus in Church Court Procedure, XI-121 pp., 1937.

109. McManus, Rev. James Edward, C.SS.R., J.C.D., The Administration of Temporal Goods in Religious Institutes, XVI-196 pp., 1937.
110. Moriarty, Rev. Eugene James, J.C.D., Oaths in Ecclesiastical Courts, X-115 pp., 1937.
111. Rainer, Rev. Eligius George, C.SS.R., J.C.D., Suspension of Clerics, XVII-249 pp., 1937.
112. Reilly, Rev. Thomas F., C.SS.R., J.C.D., Visitation of Religious, VI-195 pp., 1938.
113. Moriarity, Rev. Francis E., C.SS.R., J.C.D., The Extraordinary Absolution from Censures, XV-334 pp., 1938.
114. Connolly, Rev. Nicholas P., J.C.D., The Canonical Erection of Parishes, X-132 pp., 1938.
115. Donovan, Rev. James Joseph, J.C.D., The Pastor's Obligation in Prenuptial Investigation, XII-322 pp., 1938.
116. Harrigan, Rev. Robert J., M.A., S.T.B., J.C.D., The Radical Sanation of Invalid Marriages, VIII-208 pp., 1938.
117. Boffa, Rev. Conrad Humbert, J.C.D., Canonical Provisions for Catholic Schools, VII-211 pp., 1939.
118. Parsons, Rev. Anscar John, O.M.Cap., J.C.D., Canonical Elections, XII-236 pp., 1939.
119. Reilly, Rev. Edward Michael, A.B., J.C.D., The General Norms of Dispensation, XII-156 pp., 1939.
120. Ryan, Rev. Gerald Aloysius, A.B., J.C.D., Principles of Episcopal Jurisdiction, XII-172 pp., 1939.
121. Burton, Rev. Francis James, C.S.C., A.B., J.C.D., A Commentary on Canon 1125, X-222 pp., 1940.
122. Miaskiewicz, Rev. Francis Sigismund, J.C.D., Supplied Jurisdiction According to Canon 209, XII-340 pp., 1940.
123. Rice, Rev. Patrick William, A.B., J.C.D., Proof of Death in Prenuptial Investigation, VIII-156 pp., 1940.
124. Anglin, Rev. Thomas Francis, M.S., J.C.D., The Eucharistic Fast, VIII-183 pp., 1941.
125. Coleman, Rev. John Jerome, J.C.D., The Minister of Confirmation, VI-153 pp., 1941.
126. Downs, Rev. Joseph Emmanuel, A.B., J.C.D., The Concept of Clerical Immunity, XI-163 pp., 1941.
127. Esswein, Rev. Anthony Albert, J.C.D., Extrajudicial Penal Powers of Ecclesiastical Superiors, X-144 pp., 1941.
128. Farrell, Rev. Benjamin Francis, M.A., S.T.L., J.C.D., The Rights and Duties of the Local Ordinary Regarding Congregations of Women Religious of Pontifical Approval, V-195 pp., 1941.
129. Feeney, Rev. Thomas John, A.B., S.T.L., J.C.D., Restitutio in Integrum, VI-169 pp., 1941.
130. Findlay, Rev. Stephen William, O.S.B., A.B., J.C.D., Canonical

Norms Governing the Deposition and Degradation of Clerics, XVII-279 pp., 1941.

131. Goodwine, Rev. John, A.B., S.T.L., J.C.D., The Right of the Church to Acquire Property, VIII-119 pp., 1941.
132. Heston, Rev. Edward Louis, C.S.C., Ph.D., S.T.D., J.C.D., The Alienation of Church Property in the United States, XII-222 pp., 1941.
133. Hogan, Rev. James John, A.B., S.T.L., J.C.D., Judicial Advocates and Procurators, XIII-200 pp., 1941.
134. Kealy, Rev. Thomas M., A.B., Litt.B., J.C.D., Dowry of Women Religious, IX-152 pp., 1941.
135. Keene, Rev. Michael James, O.S.B., J.C.D., Religious Ordinaries and Canon 198, V-164 pp., 1942.
136. Kerin, Rev. Charles A., S.S., M.A., S.T.B., J.C.D., The Privation of Christian Burial, XVI-279 pp., 1941.
137. Louis, Rev. William Francis, M.A., J.C.D., Diocesan Archives, X-101 pp., 1941.
138. McDevitt, Rev. Gilbert Joseph, A.B., J.C.D., Legitimacy and Legitimation, X-247 pp., 1941.
139. McDonough, Rev. Thomas Joseph, A.B., J.C.D., Apostolic Administrators, X-217 pp., 1941.
140. Meier, Rev. Carl Anthony, A.B., J.C.D., Penal Administration Procedure Against Negligent Pastors, XI-240 pp., 1941.
141. Schmidt, Rev. John Rogg, A.B., J.C.D., The Principles of Authentic Interpretation in Canon 17 of the Code of Canon Law, XII-331 pp., 1941.
142. Slafkosky, Rev. Andrew Leonard, A.B., J.C.D., The Canonical Episcopal Visitation of the Diocese, X-197 pp., 1941.
143. Swoboda, Rev. Innocent Robert, O.F.M., J.C.D., Ignorance in Relation to the Imputability of Delicts, IX-271 pp., 1941.
144. Dubé, Rev. Arthur Joseph, A.B., J.C.D., The General Principles for the Reckoning of Time in Canon Law, VIII-299 pp., 1941.
145. McBride, Rev. James T., A.B., J.C.D., Incardination and Excardination of Seculars, XX-585 pp., 1941.
146 Król, Rev. John T., J.C.D., The Defendant in Ecclesiastical Trials, XII-207 pp., 1942.
147. Comyns, Rev. Joseph J., C.SS.R., A.B., J.C.D., Papal and Episcopal Administration of Church Property, XIV-155 pp., 1942.
148. Barry, Rev. Garrett Francis, O.M.I., J.C.D., Violation of the Cloister, XII-260 pp., 1942.
149. Bolduc, Rev. Gatien, C.S.V., A.B., S.T.L., J.C.D., Les Études dans les Religions Cléricales, VIII-155 pp., 1942.
150. Boyle, Rev. David John, M.A., J.C.D., The Juridic Effects of Moral Certitude on Pre-Nuptial Guarantees, XII-188 pp., 1942.
151. Canavan, Rev. Walter Joseph, M.A., Litt.D., J.C.D., The Profession of Faith, XII-143 pp., 1942.

152. Desrochers, Rev. Bruno, A.B., Ph.L., S.T.B., J.C.D., Le Premier Concile Plénier de Québec et le Code de Droit Canonique, XIV–186 pp., 1942.
153. Dillon, Rev. Robert Edward, A.B., J.C.D., Common Law Marriage, X-148 pp., 1942.
154. Dodwell, Rev. Edward John, Ph.D., S.T.B., J.C.D., The Time and Place for the Celebration of Marriage, X-156 pp., 1942.
155. Donnellan, Rev. Thomas Andrew, A.B., J.C.D., The Obligation of the Missa pro Populo, VII-131 pp., 1942.
156. Eltz, Rev. Louis Anthony, A.B., J.C.L., Cooperation in Crime.
157. Gass, Rev. Sylvester Francis, M.A., J.C.D., Ecclesiastical Pensions, XI-206 pp., 1942.
158. Guiniven, Rev. John Joseph, C.SS.R., J.C.D., The Precept of Hearing Mass, XIV-188 pp., 1942.
159. Gulczynski, Rev. John Theophilus, J.C.D., The Desecration and Violation of Churches, X-126 pp., 1942.
160. Hammill, Rev. John Leo, M.A., J.C.D., The Obligations of the Traveler According to Canon 14, VIII-204 pp., 1942.
161. Haydt, Rev. John Joseph, A.B., J.C.D., ,Reserved Benefices, XI-148 pp., 1942.
162. Huser, Rev. Roger John, O.F.M., A.B., J.C.D., The Crime of Abortion in Canon Law, XII-187 pp., 1942.
163. Kearney, Rev. Francis Patrick, A.B., S.T.L., J.C.L., The Principles of Canon 1127.
164. Linahen, Rev. Leo James, S.T.L., J.C.D., De Absolutione Complicis In Peccato Turpi, 114 pp., 1942.
165. McCloskey, Rev. Joseph Aloysius, A.B., J.C.D., The Subject of Ecclesiastical Law According to Canon 12, XVII-246 pp., 1942.
166. O'Neill, Rev. Francis Joseph, C.SS.R., J.C.D., The Dismissal of Religious in Temporary Vows, XIII-220 pp., 1942.
167. Prince, Rev. John Edward, A.B., S.T.D., J.C.D., The Diocesan Chancellor, X-136 pp., 1942.
168. Riesner, Rev. Albert Joseph, C.SS.R., J.C.D., Apostates and Fugitives from Religious Institutes, IX-168 pp., 1942.
169. Stenger, Rev. Joseph Bernard, J.C.D., The Mortgaging of Church Property, 186 pp., 1942.
170. Waldron, Rev. Joseph Francis, A.B., J.C.D., The Minister of Baptism, XII-197 pp., 1942.
171. Willett, Rev. Robert Albert, J.C.D., The Probative Value of Documents in Ecclesiastical Trials, X-124 pp., 1942.
172. Woeber, Rev. Edward Martin, M.A., J.C.D., The Interpellations, XII-161 pp., 1942.
173. Benko, Rev. Matthew Aloysius, O.S.B., M.A., J.C.D., The Abbot *Nullius*.

174. Christ, Rev. Joseph James, M.A., S.T.L., J.C.D., Dispensation from Vindictive Penalties.
175. Clancy, Rev. Patrick M. J., O.P., A.B., S.T.Lr., J.C.D., The Local Religious Superior, X-229 pp., 1943.
176. Clarke, Rev. Thomas James, J.C.D., Parish Societies, XII-147 pp., 1943.
177. Connolly, Rev. John Patrick, S.T.L., J.C.D., Synodal Examiners and Parish Priest Consultors, X-223 pp., 1943.
178. Drumm, Rev. William Martin, A.B., J.C.D., Hospital Chaplains.
179. Flanagan, Rev. Bernard Joseph, A.B., S.T.L., J.C.D., The Canonical Erection of Religious Houses, X-147 pp., 1943.
180. Kelleher, Rev. Stephen Joseph, A.B., S.T.B., J.C.D., Discussions with non-Catholics: Canonical Legislation, X-93 pp., 1943.
181. Lewis, Rev. Gordian, C.P., J.C.D., Chapters in Religious Institutes, XII-169 pp., 1943.
182. Marx, Rev. Adolph, J.C.D., The Declaration of Nullity of Marriages Contracted Outside the Church, X-151 pp., 1943.
183. Matulenas, Rev. Raymond Anthony, O.S.B., A.B., J.C.L., Communication, a Source of Privileges.
184. O'Leary, Rev. Charles Gerard, C.SS.R., J.C.D., Religious Dismissed After Perpetual Profession, X-213 pp., 1943.
185. Power, Rev. Cornelius Michael, J.C.D., The Blessing of Cemeteries.
186. Shuhler, Rev. Ralph Vincent, O.S.A., J.C.D., Privileges of Regulars to Absolve and Dispense, XII-195 pp., 1943.
187. Ziolkowski, Rev. Thaddeus Stanislaus, A.B., J.C.D., The Consecration and Blessing of Churches, XII-151 pp., 1943.
188. Heneghan, Rev. John Joseph, S.T.D., J.C.D., The Marriages of Unworthy Catholics: Canons 1065 and 1066.
189. Carroll, Rev. Coleman Francis, M.A., S.T.L., J.C.L., Charitable Institutions.
190. Ciesluk, Rev. Joseph Edward, Ph.B., S.T.L., J.C.L., National Parishes in the United States.
191. Coburn, Rev. Vincent Paul, A.B., J.C.L., Marriages of Conscience.
192. Connors, Rev. Charles Paul, C.S.Sp., A.B., J.C.L., Extra-Judicial Procurators in the Code of Canon Law.
193. Coyle, Rev. Paul Raymond, A.B., J.C.L., Judicial Exceptions.
194. Fair, Rev. Bartholomew Francis, A.B., S.T.L., J.C.L., The Impediment of Abduction.
195. Gallagher, Rev. Thomas Raphael, O.P., A.B., S.T.Lr., J.C.L., The Examination of the Qualities of the Ordinand.
196. Gannon, Rev. John Mark, S.T.L., J.C.L., The Interstices Required for the Promotion to Orders.
197. Goldsmith, Rev. J. William, B.C.S., S.T.L., J.C.L., The Competence of Church and State over Marriage—Disputed Points.

198. Goodwine, Rev. Joseph Gerard, A.B., S.T.B., J.C.L., The Reception of Converts.
199. Kowalski, Rev. Romuald Eugene, O.F.M., A.B., J.C.L., Sustenance of Religious Houses of Regulars.
200. McCoy, Rev. Alan Edward, O.F.M., J.C.L., Force and Fear in Relation to Delictual Imputability and Penal Responsibility.
201. McDevitt, Rev. Vincent John, Ph.B., S.T.L., J.C.L., Perjury.
202. Martin, Rev. Thomas Owen, Ph.D., S.T.D., J.C.L., Adverse Possession, Prescription and Limitation of Actions: The Canonical "Praescriptio."
203. Miklosovic, Rev. Paul John, A.B., J.C.L., Attempted Marriages and Their Consequent Juridic Effects.
204. Mundy, Rev. Thomas Maurice, A.B., S.T.L., J.C.L., The Union of Parishes.
205. O'Dea, Rev. John Coyle, A.B., J.C.L., The Matrimonial Impediment of Nonage.
206. Olalia, Rev. Alexander Ayson, S.T.L., J.C.L., A Comparative Study of the Christian Constitution of States and the Constitution of the Philippine Commonwealth.
207. Poisson, Rev. Pierre-Marie, C.S.C., A.B., Ph.L., Th.L., J.C.L., Droits Patrimoniaux des Maisons et des Églises Religieuses.
208. Stadalnikas, Rev. Casimir Joseph, M.I.C., J.C.L., Reservation of Censures.
209. Sullivan, Rev. Eugene Henry, S.T.L., J.C.L., Proof of the Reception of the Sacraments.
210. Vaughan, Rev. William Edward, J.C.L., Constitutions for Diocesan Courts.
211. Lyons, Rev. Joseph Henry, J.C.L., The Joinder of Issue in Canonical Trials.

www.ingramcontent.com/pod-product-compliance
Lightning Source LLC
LaVergne TN
LVHW050207080826
844660LV00012B/369

* 9 7 8 0 8 1 3 2 2 3 8 9 6 *